Curriculum Focal Points *for* Prekindergarten *through* Grade 8 Mathematics

Curriculum Focal Points *for* Prekindergarten *through* Grade 8 Mathematics

A Quest for Coherence

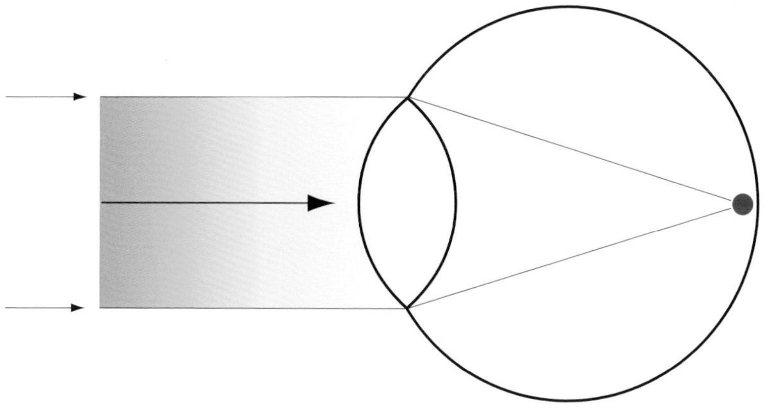

Library of Congress Cataloging-in-Publication Data

National Council of Teachers of Mathematics.
Curriculum focal points for prekindergarten through grade 8 mathematics : a quest for coherence / National Council of Teachers of Mathematics.
p. cm.
Includes bibliographical references.
ISBN 0-87353-595-2
1. Mathematics—Study and teaching—United States—Evaluation. 2. Curriculum evaluation. I. Title.
QA13.N365 2006
372.7043—dc22

2006019201

The National Council of Teachers of Mathematics is a public voice of mathematics education, providing vision, leadership, and professional development to support teachers in ensuring mathematics learning of the highest quality for all students.

Curriculum Focal Points for Prekindergarten through Grade 8 Mathematics: A Quest for Coherence is an official position of the National Council of Teachers of Mathematics as approved by its Board of Directors, April 2006.

Printed in the United States of America

Table of Contents

Preface

As states and local school districts implement more rigorous assessment and accountability systems, teachers often face long lists of mathematics topics or learning expectations to address at each grade level, with many topics repeating from year to year. Lacking clear, consistent priorities and focus, teachers stretch to find the time to present important mathematical topics effectively and in depth.

The National Council of Teachers of Mathematics (NCTM) is responding to this challenge by presenting *Curriculum Focal Points for Prekindergarten through Grade 8 Mathematics: A Quest for Coherence.* Building on *Principles and Standards for School Mathematics* (NCTM 2000), this new publication is offered as a starting point in a dialogue on what is important at particular levels of instruction and as an initial step toward a more coherent, focused curriculum in this country.

The writing team for *Curriculum Focal Points for Prekindergarten through Grade 8 Mathematics* consisted of nine members, with at least one university-level mathematics educator or mathematician and one pre-K–8 classroom practitioner from each of the three grade bands (pre-K–grade 2, grades 3–5, and grades 6–8). The writing team examined curricula from multiple states and countries as well as a wide array of researchers' and experts' writings in creating a set of focal points for pre-K–grade 8 mathematics.

On behalf of the Board of Directors, we thank everyone who helped make this publication possible.

Cathy Seeley
President, 2004–2006
National Council of Teachers of Mathematics

Francis (Skip) Fennell
President, 2006–2008
National Council of Teachers of Mathematics

Members of the Writing Team

Jane F. Schielack, *Chair,* Texas A&M University, College Station, Texas
Sybilla Beckman, University of Georgia, Athens, Georgia
Randall I. Charles, San José State University (emeritus), San José, California
Douglas H. Clements, University at Buffalo, State University of New York, Buffalo, New York
Paula B. Duckett, District of Columbia Public Schools (retired), Washington, D.C.
Francis (Skip) Fennell, McDaniel College, Westminster, Maryland
Sharon L. Lewandowski, Bryant Woods Elementary School, Columbia, Maryland
Emma Treviño, Charles A. Dana Center, University of Texas at Austin, Austin, Texas
Rose Mary Zbiek, The Pennsylvania State University, University Park, Pennsylvania

Staff Liaison
Melanie S. Ott, National Council of Teachers of Mathematics, Reston, Virginia

Acknowledgments

Drafts of *Curriculum Focal Points for Prekindergarten through Grade 8 Mathematics: A Quest for Coherence* were shared with a diverse group of mathematicians, mathematics educators, curriculum developers, policymakers, and classroom practitioners, who provided formal reviews. In addition, many other individuals and collegial groups committed to improving pre-K–12 mathematics teaching and learning offered their perceptions and comments informally. The Board of Directors and the writing team are grateful to all the reviewers who shared their expertise. The comments of the reviewers do not constitute endorsement of the final document.

We extend sincere thanks to the following individuals, who offered their insights, perspectives, and advice in formal reviews of the first draft of *Curriculum Focal Points for Prekindergarten through Grade 8 Mathematics.* Their diverse commentary provided helpful guidance that made the final publication stronger, clearer, and more meaningful.

David Bressoud, Macalester College, St. Paul, Minnesota

William Bush, University of Louisville, Louisville, Kentucky

Anne Collins, Lesley University, Cambridge, Massachuettes

Joan Ferrini-Mundy, Michigan State University, East Lansing, Michigan

Linda Gojak, John Carroll University, University Heights, Ohio

Jeremy Kilpatrick, University of Georgia, Athens, Georgia

Denise Mewborn, University of Georgia, Athens, Georgia

Anne Mikesell, Ohio Department of Education (retired), Columbus, Ohio

R. James Milgram, Stanford University, Stanford, California

Barbara Reys, University of Missouri–Columbia, Columbia, Missouri

J. Michael Shaughnessy, Portland State University, Portland, Oregon

Norma Torres-Martinez, Texas Education Agency, Austin, Texas

Norman Webb, University of Wisconsin–Madison, Madison, Wisconsin

Barbara G. Wells, University of California, Los Angeles (UCLA), Los Angeles, California

We also offer thanks to the following individuals, who examined various versions of the manuscript and commented informally:

Nancy Acconciamessa
Susan Addington
Richard Askey
Deborah Loewenberg Ball
Thomas Banchoff
Hyman Bass
Michael T. Battista
Gail Burrill
John Carter
Dinah Chancellor
Al Cuoco
Jerome Dancis
Valerie DeBellis
Cathie Dillender
John Dossey
Jerry Dwyer
Karen Fuson
E. Paul Goldenberg
Eric Hart
Wayne Harvey
David W. Henderson
Cheryl Hlavsa
Roger Howe
Susan Hudson Hull
Lisa Kasmer
Catherine Kelly
Cliff Konold
Glenda Lappan
Steve Leinwand
Mary Lindquist
Johnny Lott
Frank Marburger
Robert McIntosh
Gregg McMann
Debbie Nix
Jana Palmer
Caroline Piangerelli
Gerald R. Rising
Joseph Rosenstein
Susan Jo Russell
Yoram Sagher
Kay B. Sammons
Richard Schaar
Janet K. Scheer
William Schmidt
Marjorie Senechal
Nina Shteingold
Dorothy Strong
Maria Terrell
John Van de Walle
Patsy Wang-Iverson
Virginia M. Warfield
Donna Watts
Iris Weiss
Grayson H. Wheatley
W. Stephen Wilson

Introduction

In 1980 the National Council of Teachers of Mathematics (NCTM) published *An Agenda for Action* (NCTM 1980), launching an era of bold professional outreach by describing the shape that school mathematics programs should take. That publication outlined ten recommendations for K–12 mathematics programs, focusing on the fundamental need of students to learn how to solve problems. In 1989, the Council published *Curriculum and Evaluation Standards for School Mathematics* (NCTM 1989), expanding these recommendations into a vision for mathematics teaching and learning in K–grade 4, grades 5–8, and grades 9–12. *Curriculum and Evaluation Standards* provided major direction for states and school districts in developing their curriculum guidelines. *Principles and Standards for School Mathematics* (NCTM 2000) followed at the turn of the new century, adding underlying principles for school mathematics and clarifying and elaborating on the 1989 Standards for pre-K–grade 2, grades 3–5, grades 6–8, and grades 9–12.

Principles and Standards for School Mathematics remains the comprehensive reference on developing mathematical knowledge across the grades, and the Council continues to produce numerous related publications and services to support, expand, and illuminate this work. *Curriculum Focal Points for Prekindergarten through Grade 8 Mathematics: A Quest for Coherence* extends the Council's leadership of more than twenty-five years by describing an approach to curriculum development that focuses on areas of emphasis within each grade from prekindergarten through grade 8.

An approach that focuses on a small number of significant mathematical "targets" for each grade level offers a way of thinking about what is important in school mathematics that is different from commonly accepted notions of goals, standards, objectives, or learning expectations. These more conventional structures tend to result in lists of very specific items grouped under general headings. By contrast, *Curriculum Focal Points for Prekindergarten through Grade 8 Mathematics* offers more than headings for long lists, providing instead descriptions of the most significant mathematical concepts and skills at each grade level. Organizing a curriculum around these described focal points, with a clear emphasis on the processes that *Principles and Standards* addresses in the Process Standards—communication, reasoning, representation, connections, and, particularly, problem solving—can provide students with a connected, coherent, ever expanding body of mathematical knowledge and ways of thinking. Such a comprehensive mathematics experience can prepare students for whatever career or professional path they may choose as well as equip them to solve many problems that they will face in the future.

The curriculum focal points presented here offer both immediate and long-term opportunities for improving the teaching and learning of mathematics. They provide ideas that may kindle fruitful discussions among teacher leaders and teachers about areas to emphasize as they consider the developmental needs of their students and examine a year's program of instruction. Teachers might also see opportunities to develop or select lessons that bring together related topics in meaningful contexts to reinforce or extend the most important connections, understandings, and skills. The long-term opportunity, however, is for mathematics leaders at every level to use *Curriculum Focal Points for Prekindergarten through Grade 8 Mathematics* to launch an ongoing, far-reaching, significant discussion with the potential to guide the thinking of the profession in the development of the next generation of curriculum standards, textbooks, and tests. This work may assist in the creation and eventual development of new models for defining curriculum, organizing instruction, developing materials, and creating meaningful assessments that can help students learn critical mathematical skills, processes, and ways of thinking and can measure and communicate what students know about the mathematics that we expect them to learn.

Curriculum Focal Points for Prekindergarten through Grade 8 Mathematics thus represents an important, initial step in advancing collaborative discussions about what mathematics students should know and be able to do. Use the focal points presented here to guide discussions as you review, refine, and revise mathematics curricula. Take this opportunity to share the best that we know as we work together to produce improved tools that support our shared goal of a high-quality mathematics education for every student.

1

Why Identify Curriculum Focal Points?

The National Council of Teachers of Mathematics produced *Principles and Standards for School Mathematics* (NCTM 2000) to update and extend the recommendations for learning and teaching mathematics that had appeared in *Curriculum and Evaluation Standards for School Mathematics* (NCTM 1989), *Professional Standards for Teaching Mathematics* (NCTM 1991), and *Assessment Standards for School Mathematics* (NCTM 1995). *Principles and Standards* enunciated the Curriculum Principle, which states, "A curriculum is more than a collection of activities: it must be coherent, focused on important mathematics, and well articulated across the grades" (p. 14). Specifically, "a well-articulated curriculum gives teachers guidance regarding important ideas or major themes, which receive special attention at different points in time. It also gives guidance about the depth of study warranted at particular times and when closure is expected for particular skills or concepts" (p. 16).

This definition of curriculum articulation echoes a central question that occupies state and local leaders in mathematics education: *What mathematics should be the focus of instruction and learning at particular grade levels of the pre-K–12 educational system?* As *Principles and Standards* states, "Those who design curriculum frameworks, assessments, instructional materials, and classroom instruction based on *Principles and Standards* will need to make their own decisions about emphasis and order" (p. 31). *Curriculum Focal Points for Prekindergarten through Grade 8 Mathematics* provides one possible response to the question of how to organize curriculum standards within a coherent, focused curriculum, by showing how to build on important mathematical content and connections identified for each grade level, pre-K–8.

Inconsistency in the Placement of Topics by Grade Level in U.S. Mathematics Curricula

Analysis of curricula of countries participating in the Third International Mathematics and Science Study (TIMSS [1997]; now known as the Trends in International Mathematics and Science Study) led to the familiar description of school mathematics in the United States as "a mile wide and an inch deep" (Schmidt, McKnight, and Raizen 1997). In addition, research on the curricular expectations of states and school systems across the country indicates inconsistency in the grade placements of mathematics topics, as well as in how they are defined and what students are expected to learn.

State and local districts, with varying resources for providing leadership in mathematics education, have been working fairly independently to develop student learning expectations, as required by the federal law No Child Left Behind (2002). The result has been a wide variety of mathematics curriculum standards, with little consensus on the placement or emphasis of topics within specific grade levels (Reys et al. 2005). For example, in a study of the mathematics curriculum standards of ten states (Reys et al. 2006), the total number of grade-level expectations in mathematics for grade 4 ranged from 26 to 89 (see table 1).

Table 1. Number of Fourth-Grade Learning Expectations (LEs) per State by Content Strand (from Reys et al. 2006, p. 20)

	Number & Operations	Geometry	Measurement	Algebra	Data Analysis, Prob & Stat	Total Number of LEs
California	16	11	4	7	5	43
Texas	15	7	3	4	3	32
New York	27	8	10	5	6	56
Florida	31	11	17	10	20	89
Ohio	15	8	6	6	13	48
Michigan	37	5	11	0	3	56
New Jersey	21	10	8	6	11	56
North Carolina	14	3	2	3	4	26
Georgia	23	10	5	3	4	45
Virginia	17	8	11	2	3	41

The Importance of Curricular Focus in Mathematics

Many factors have contributed to the need for a common mathematical focus for each grade level, pre-K–8. These include the increased emphasis on accountability testing, high levels of mobility of both students and teachers, and greater costs of curriculum development. A focused, coherent mathematics curriculum with a national scope has the potential to ease the impact of widely varying learning and assessment expectations on both students and teachers who relocate. In addition, a focused curriculum would allow teachers to commit more time each year to topics receiving special emphasis. At the same time, students would have opportunities to explore these topics in depth, in the context of related content and connected applications, thus developing more robust mathematical understandings.

In a survey of employees of forty-seven educational agencies—those responsible for improving curriculum and instruction in their states—85 percent of the respondents indicated that "national leadership is needed to assist in future articulation of learning expectations in mathematics, particularly from national professional organizations of mathematics teachers (K–12 and university) and mathematicians" (Reys et al. 2005, p. 17). This publication addresses that need.

2

What Are Curriculum Focal Points?

Curriculum focal points are important mathematical topics for each grade level, pre-K–8. These areas of instructional emphasis can serve as organizing structures for curriculum design and instruction at and across grade levels. The topics are central to mathematics: they convey knowledge and skills that are essential to educated citizens, and they provide the foundations for further mathematical learning. Because the focal points are core structures that lay a conceptual foundation, they can serve to organize content, connecting and bringing coherence to multiple concepts and processes taught at and across grade levels. They are indispensable elements in developing problem solving, reasoning, and critical thinking skills, which are important to all mathematics learning.

When instruction focuses on a small number of key areas of emphasis, students gain extended experience with core concepts and skills. Such experience can facilitate deep understanding, mathematical fluency, and an ability to generalize. The decision to organize instruction around focal points assumes that the learning of mathematics is cumulative, with work in the later grades building on and deepening what students have learned in the earlier grades, without repetitious and inefficient reteaching. A curriculum built on focal points also has the potential to offer opportunities for the diagnosis of difficulties and immediate intervention, thus helping students who are struggling with important mathematics content.

What characteristics qualify a concept or topic to be a curriculum focal point? For inclusion in *Curriculum Focal Points for Prekindergarten through Grade 8 Mathematics*, a focal point had to pass three rigorous tests:

- Is it mathematically important, both for further study in mathematics and for use in applications in and outside of school?
- Does it "fit" with what is known about learning mathematics?
- Does it connect logically with the mathematics in earlier and later grade levels?

A curriculum focal point may draw on several connected mathematical content topics described in *Principles and Standards for School Mathematics* (NCTM 2000). It should be addressed by students in the context of the mathematical processes of problem solving, reasoning and proof, communication, connections, and representation. Without facility with these critical processes, a student's mathematical knowledge is likely to be fragile and limited in its usefulness.

A complete set of curriculum focal points, situated within the processes of mathematics, can provide an outline of an integrated mathematics curriculum that is different from the outline created by a set of grade-level mastery objectives or a list of separated content and process targets. In contrast with grade-level mastery objectives, which can be interpreted as endpoints for learning, curriculum focal points are clearly areas of emphasis, calling for instruction that will help students learn content that gives them a foundation for increasing their understanding as they encounter richer and more challenging mathematics.

Instruction based on focal points would devote the vast majority of attention to the content identified for special emphasis in a grade. A curriculum for pre-K–8 based on a connected set of such focal points could provide a solid mathematical foundation for high school mathematics.

3

How Should Curriculum Focal Points Be Used?

Curriculum Focal Points for Prekindergarten through Grade 8 Mathematics highlights important mathematics at particular grade levels for the use of those who are responsible for the development of mathematics curricula, standards, and assessment—primarily the mathematics education leaders and policymakers at the national, state, and local levels. As a result of the wide variation in the placement of topics in current mathematics curricula (Reys et al. 2006), the grade-level designations of particular curriculum focal points in this publication may not match the placement of the corresponding content in an existing curriculum. This publication is presented as a framework on which the next generation of state and district-level mathematics curricula might be built. Organizational strategies that embody the field's best thinking, such as these focal points, can serve as a catalyst to curriculum development and positively influence the design of materials for instruction and assessment.

The set of curriculum focal points described here represents an attempt to provide curriculum developers with a clear organizational model for establishing a mathematics curriculum from prekindergarten through grade 8 by identifying for each grade level important content that can build connected and integrated mathematical understanding. The curriculum focal points and their accompanying "connections" to related content outline instructional targets for a basic, integrated, grade-by-grade framework for a coherent mathematics curriculum.

Curriculum Focal Points for Prekindergarten through Grade 8 Mathematics does not specify instructional approaches for the implementation of the suggested curriculum focal points. Its presentations of the focal points include neither suggestions for tools to use in teaching nor recommendations for professional development in content or pedagogy. The focal points cannot be used alone as lesson plans. Nor do they answer the question, "What should I do in class on Monday?" Nevertheless, the curriculum focal points identified here should be of considerable interest to teachers and other practitioners, as well as curriculum developers and policymakers.

To achieve the best results with students when teaching for the depth, understanding, and proficiency sought by the curriculum focal points, teachers themselves will need a deep understanding of the mathematics and facility with the relationships among mathematical ideas. Thus, effective instruction built on the curriculum focal points requires in-depth preparation of preservice teachers and ongoing professional development for in-service teachers.

4

How Do the Curriculum Focal Points Relate to *Principles and Standards for School Mathematics*?

Principles and Standards for School Mathematics (NCTM 2000) describes the foundational mathematical ideas on which the focal points in *Curriculum Focal Points for Prekindergarten through Grade 8 Mathematics* rest and toward which they direct students' learning. *Principles and Standards* remains the definitive reference on the development of mathematical content and processes across the grades. Since the publication of this influential work in 2000, ideas like *coherence, focus, high expectations, computational fluency, representation,* and *important mathematics* have become regular elements in discussions about improving school mathematics, and thinking about these ideas has evolved considerably. As the next step in devising resources to support the development of a coherent curriculum, NCTM now offers a new publication, with a set of curriculum focal points and connections for mathematics education in prekindergarten through grade 8.

Principles and Standards includes a thorough discussion of the necessity for learning mathematical content through the processes of problem solving, reasoning and proof, communication, connections, and representation. Although some of these processes may be evident in the descriptions of particular focal points, this new publication primarily targets *content.* Its presentation of curriculum focal points assumes that the mathematical processes described in *Principles and Standards* will be implemented in instruction that requires students to discuss and validate their mathematical thinking; create and analyze a variety of representations that illuminate the connections within the mathematics; and apply the mathematics that they are learning in solving problems, judging claims, and making decisions.

Curriculum Focal Points for Prekindergarten through Grade 8 Mathematics identifies three focal points at each grade level. Each set of three focal points, together with the integrated content taught in the context of the processes, should encompass the major portion of instruction at that grade level. The presentations of the focal points for each grade level also identify "Connections to the Focal Points" in a column at the right. These connections serve two purposes:

1. They recognize the need for introductory and continuing experiences related to focal points identified for other grade levels.
2. They identify ways in which a grade level's focal points can support learning in relation to strands that are not focal points at that grade level.

The "Connections to the Focal Points" column for each grade level brings in other important topics in meaningful ways. For example, the grade 2 "Connections" highlight the fact that the Measurement Focal Point for grade 2 ("Developing an understanding of linear measurement and facility in measuring lengths") includes work with applications and models using the shapes from the Geometry Focal Point for grade 1 ("Composing and decomposing geometric shapes"). At the same time, students in grade 2 continue to use vocabulary and spatial reasoning that will be essential for learning the content specified in the Geometry Focal Point for grade 3 ("Describing and analyzing properties of two-dimensional shapes"). Because a curriculum that is integrated and internally connected in this way uses related concepts and skills to support and enrich one or more focal points at a grade level, it has the potential to maximize students' learning.

Each focal point in this publication takes its name from the content strand or strands to which it relates in *Principles and Standards for School Mathematics.* Many focal points relate to more than one content strand, highlighting the integrated nature of the curriculum focal points. That single focal points are often described with a combination of items from different content strands in *Principles and Standards* reflects the fact that *Principles and Standards* itself presents "a connected body of mathematical understandings and competencies ... rather than a menu from which to make curricular choices" (p. 29). Color-coded comparison charts in the appendix illustrate the extent to which the curriculum focal points and their connections include content that *Principles and Standards* expects instruction to address in the corresponding grade bands.

5

Curriculum Focal Points for Mathematics in Prekindergarten through Grade 8

Three curriculum focal points are identified and described for each grade level, pre-K–8, along with connections to guide integration of the focal points at that grade level and across grade levels, to form a comprehensive mathematics curriculum. To build students' strength in the use of mathematical processes, instruction in these content areas should incorporate—

- the use of the mathematics to solve problems;
- an application of logical reasoning to justify procedures and solutions; and
- an involvement in the design and analysis of multiple representations to learn, make connections among, and communicate about the ideas within and outside of mathematics.

The purpose of identifying these grade-level curriculum focal points and connections is to enable students to learn the content in the context of a focused and cohesive curriculum that implements problem solving, reasoning, and critical thinking.

These curriculum focal points should be considered as major instructional goals and desirable learning expectations, not as a list of objectives for students to master. They should be implemented with the intention of building mathematical competency for all students, bolstered by the pedagogical understanding that not every student learns at the same rate or acquires concepts and skills at the same time.

Those who are involved in curriculum planning for grades 6–8 should note that this set of curriculum focal points has been designed with the intention of providing a three-year middle school program that includes a full year of general mathematics in each of grades 6, 7, and 8. Those whose programs offer an algebra course in grade 8 (or earlier) should consider including the curriculum focal points that this framework calls for in grade 8 in grade 6 or grade 7. Alternatively, these topics could be incorporated into the high school program. Either way, curricula would not omit the important content that the grade 7 and grade 8 focal points offer students in preparation for algebra and for their long-term mathematical knowledge.

Curriculum Focal Points and Connections for Prekindergarten

The set of three curriculum focal points and related connections for mathematics in prekindergarten follow. These topics are the recommended content emphases for this grade level. It is essential that these focal points be addressed in contexts that promote problem solving, reasoning, communication, making connections, and designing and analyzing representations.

Prekindergarten Curriculum Focal Points	Connections to the Focal Points
***Number and Operations:* Developing an understanding of whole numbers, including concepts of correspondence, counting, cardinality, and comparison** Children develop an understanding of the meanings of whole numbers and recognize the number of objects in small groups without counting and by counting—the first and most basic mathematical algorithm. They understand that number words refer to quantity. They use one-to-one correspondence to solve problems by matching sets and comparing number amounts and in counting objects to 10 and beyond. They understand that the last word that they state in counting tells "how many," they count to determine number amounts and compare quantities (using language such as "more than" and "less than"), and they order sets by the number of objects in them.	***Data Analysis:*** Children learn the foundations of data analysis by using objects' attributes that they have identified in relation to geometry and measurement (e.g., size, quantity, orientation, number of sides or vertices, color) for various purposes, such as describing, sorting, or comparing. For example, children sort geometric figures by shape, compare objects by weight ("heavier," "lighter"), or describe sets of objects by the number of objects in each set. ***Number and Operations:*** Children use meanings of numbers to create strategies for solving problems and responding to practical situations, such as getting just enough napkins for a group, or mathematical situations, such as determining that any shape is a triangle if it has exactly three straight sides and is closed. ***Algebra:*** Children recognize and duplicate simple sequential patterns (e.g., square, circle, square, circle, square, circle,...).
***Geometry:* Identifying shapes and describing spatial relationships** Children develop spatial reasoning by working from two perspectives on space as they examine the shapes of objects and inspect their relative positions. They find shapes in their environments and describe them in their own words. They build pictures and designs by combining two- and three-dimensional shapes, and they solve such problems as deciding which piece will fit into a space in a puzzle. They discuss the relative positions of objects with vocabulary such as "above," "below," and "next to."	
***Measurement:* Identifying measurable attributes and comparing objects by using these attributes** Children identify objects as "the same" or "different," and then "more" or "less," on the basis of attributes that they can measure. They identify measurable attributes such as length and weight and solve problems by making direct comparisons of objects on the basis of those attributes.	

Curriculum Focal Points and Connections for Kindergarten

The set of three curriculum focal points and related connections for mathematics in kindergarten follow. These topics are the recommended content emphases for this grade level. It is essential that these focal points be addressed in contexts that promote problem solving, reasoning, communication, making connections, and designing and analyzing representations.

Kindergarten Curriculum Focal Points	Connections to the Focal Points
***Number and Operations:* Representing, comparing, and ordering whole numbers and joining and separating sets** Children use numbers, including written numerals, to represent quantities and to solve quantitative problems, such as counting objects in a set, creating a set with a given number of objects, comparing and ordering sets or numerals by using both cardinal and ordinal meanings, and modeling simple joining and separating situations with objects. They choose, combine, and apply effective strategies for answering quantitative questions, including quickly recognizing the number in a small set, counting and producing sets of given sizes, counting the number in combined sets, and counting backward.	***Data Analysis:*** Children sort objects and use one or more attributes to solve problems. For example, they might sort solids that roll easily from those that do not. Or they might collect data and use counting to answer such questions as, "What is our favorite snack?" They re-sort objects by using new attributes (e.g., after sorting solids according to which ones roll, they might re-sort the solids according to which ones stack easily). ***Geometry:*** Children integrate their understandings of geometry, measurement, and number. For example, they understand, discuss, and create simple navigational directions (e.g., "Walk forward 10 steps, turn right, and walk forward 5 steps"). ***Algebra:*** Children identify, duplicate, and extend simple number patterns and sequential and growing patterns (e.g., patterns made with shapes) as preparation for creating rules that describe relationships.
***Geometry:* Describing shapes and space** Children interpret the physical world with geometric ideas (e.g., shape, orientation, spatial relations) and describe it with corresponding vocabulary. They identify, name, and describe a variety of shapes, such as squares, triangles, circles, rectangles, (regular) hexagons, and (isosceles) trapezoids presented in a variety of ways (e.g., with different sizes or orientations), as well as such three-dimensional shapes as spheres, cubes, and cylinders. They use basic shapes and spatial reasoning to model objects in their environment and to construct more complex shapes.	
***Measurement:* Ordering objects by measurable attributes** Children use measurable attributes, such as length or weight, to solve problems by comparing and ordering objects. They compare the lengths of two objects both directly (by comparing them with each other) and indirectly (by comparing both with a third object), and they order several objects according to length.	

Curriculum Focal Points and Connections for Grade 1

The set of three curriculum focal points and related connections for mathematics in grade 1 follow. These topics are the recommended content emphases for this grade level. It is essential that these focal points be addressed in contexts that promote problem solving, reasoning, communication, making connections, and designing and analyzing representations.

Grade 1 Curriculum Focal Points	Connections to the Focal Points
***Number and Operations* and *Algebra:* Developing understandings of addition and subtraction and strategies for basic addition facts and related subtraction facts** Children develop strategies for adding and subtracting whole numbers on the basis of their earlier work with small numbers. They use a variety of models, including discrete objects, length-based models (e.g., lengths of connecting cubes), and number lines, to model "part-whole," "adding to," "taking away from," and "comparing" situations to develop an understanding of the meanings of addition and subtraction and strategies to solve such arithmetic problems. Children understand the connections between counting and the operations of addition and subtraction (e.g., adding two is the same as "counting on" two). They use properties of addition (commutativity and associativity) to add whole numbers, and they create and use increasingly sophisticated strategies based on these properties (e.g., "making tens") to solve addition and subtraction problems involving basic facts. By comparing a variety of solution strategies, children relate addition and subtraction as inverse operations.	***Number and Operations* and *Algebra:*** Children use mathematical reasoning, including ideas such as commutativity and associativity and beginning ideas of tens and ones, to solve two-digit addition and subtraction problems with strategies that they understand and can explain. They solve both routine and nonroutine problems. ***Measurement* and *Data Analysis:*** Children strengthen their sense of number by solving problems involving measurements and data. Measuring by laying multiple copies of a unit end to end and then counting the units by using groups of tens and ones supports children's understanding of number lines and number relationships. Representing measurements and discrete data in picture and bar graphs involves counting and comparisons that provide another meaningful connection to number relationships. ***Algebra:*** Through identifying, describing, and applying number patterns and properties in developing strategies for basic facts, children learn about other properties of numbers and operations, such as odd and even (e.g., "Even numbers of objects can be paired, with none left over"), and 0 as the identity element for addition.
***Number and Operations:* Developing an understanding of whole number relationships, including grouping in tens and ones** Children compare and order whole numbers (at least to 100) to develop an understanding of and solve problems involving the relative sizes of these numbers. They think of whole numbers between 10 and 100 in terms of groups of tens and ones (especially recognizing the numbers 11 to 19 as 1 group of ten and particular numbers of ones). They understand the sequential order of the counting numbers and their relative magnitudes and represent numbers on a number line.	
***Geometry:* Composing and decomposing geometric shapes** Children compose and decompose plane and solid figures (e.g., by putting two congruent isosceles triangles together to make a rhombus), thus building an understanding of part-whole relationships as well as the properties of the original and composite shapes. As they combine figures, they recognize them from different perspectives and orientations, describe their geometric attributes and properties, and determine how they are alike and different, in the process developing a background for measurement and initial understandings of such properties as congruence and symmetry.	

Curriculum Focal Points and Connections for Grade 2

The set of three curriculum focal points and related connections for mathematics in grade 2 follow. These topics are the recommended content emphases for this grade level. It is essential that these focal points be addressed in contexts that promote problem solving, reasoning, communication, making connections, and designing and analyzing representations.

Grade 2 Curriculum Focal Points

Number and Operations: **Developing an understanding of the base-ten numeration system and place-value concepts**

Children develop an understanding of the base-ten numeration system and place-value concepts (at least to 1000). Their understanding of base-ten numeration includes ideas of counting in units and multiples of hundreds, tens, and ones, as well as a grasp of number relationships, which they demonstrate in a variety of ways, including comparing and ordering numbers. They understand multidigit numbers in terms of place value, recognizing that place-value notation is a shorthand for the sums of multiples of powers of 10 (e.g., 853 as 8 hundreds + 5 tens + 3 ones).

Number and Operations **and** ***Algebra:*** **Developing quick recall of addition facts and related subtraction facts and fluency with multidigit addition and subtraction**

Children use their understanding of addition to develop quick recall of basic addition facts and related subtraction facts. They solve arithmetic problems by applying their understanding of models of addition and subtraction (such as combining or separating sets or using number lines), relationships and properties of number (such as place value), and properties of addition (commutativity and associativity). Children develop, discuss, and use efficient, accurate, and generalizable methods to add and subtract multidigit whole numbers. They select and apply appropriate methods to estimate sums and differences or calculate them mentally, depending on the context and numbers involved. They develop fluency with efficient procedures, including standard algorithms, for adding and subtracting whole numbers, understand why the procedures work (on the basis of place value and properties of operations), and use them to solve problems.

Measurement: **Developing an understanding of linear measurement and facility in measuring lengths**

Children develop an understanding of the meaning and processes of measurement, including such underlying concepts as partitioning (the mental activity of slicing the length of an object into equal-sized units) and transitivity (e.g., if object A is longer than object B and object B is longer than object C, then object A is longer than object C). They understand linear measure as an iteration of units and use rulers and other measurement tools with that understanding. They understand the need for equal-length units, the use of standard units of measure (centimeter and inch), and the inverse relationship between the size of a unit and the number of units used in a particular measurement (i.e., children recognize that the smaller the unit, the more iterations they need to cover a given length).

Connections to the Focal Points

Number and Operations: Children use place value and properties of operations to create equivalent representations of given numbers (such as 35 represented by 35 ones, 3 tens and 5 ones, or 2 tens and 15 ones) and to write, compare, and order multidigit numbers. They use these ideas to compose and decompose multidigit numbers. Children add and subtract to solve a variety of problems, including applications involving measurement, geometry, and data, as well as nonroutine problems. In preparation for grade 3, they solve problems involving multiplicative situations, developing initial understandings of multiplication as repeated addition.

Geometry and ***Measurement:*** Children estimate, measure, and compute lengths as they solve problems involving data, space, and movement through space. By composing and decomposing two-dimensional shapes (intentionally substituting arrangements of smaller shapes for larger shapes or substituting larger shapes for many smaller shapes), they use geometric knowledge and spatial reasoning to develop foundations for understanding area, fractions, and proportions.

Algebra: Children use number patterns to extend their knowledge of properties of numbers and operations. For example, when skip counting, they build foundations for understanding multiples and factors.

Curriculum Focal Points and Connections for Grade 3

The set of three curriculum focal points and related connections for mathematics in grade 3 follow. These topics are the recommended content emphases for this grade level. It is essential that these focal points be addressed in contexts that promote problem solving, reasoning, communication, making connections, and designing and analyzing representations.

Grade 3 Curriculum Focal Points	Connections to the Focal Points
***Number and Operations* and *Algebra:* Developing understandings of multiplication and division and strategies for basic multiplication facts and related division facts** Students understand the meanings of multiplication and division of whole numbers through the use of representations (e.g., equal-sized groups, arrays, area models, and equal "jumps" on number lines for multiplication, and successive subtraction, partitioning, and sharing for division). They use properties of addition and multiplication (e.g., commutativity, associativity, and the distributive property) to multiply whole numbers and apply increasingly sophisticated strategies based on these properties to solve multiplication and division problems involving basic facts. By comparing a variety of solution strategies, students relate multiplication and division as inverse operations. ***Number and Operations:* Developing an understanding of fractions and fraction equivalence** Students develop an understanding of the meanings and uses of fractions to represent parts of a whole, parts of a set, or points or distances on a number line. They understand that the size of a fractional part is relative to the size of the whole, and they use fractions to represent numbers that are equal to, less than, or greater than 1. They solve problems that involve comparing and ordering fractions by using models, benchmark fractions, or common numerators or denominators. They understand and use models, including the number line, to identify equivalent fractions. ***Geometry:* Describing and analyzing properties of two-dimensional shapes** Students describe, analyze, compare, and classify two-dimensional shapes by their sides and angles and connect these attributes to definitions of shapes. Students investigate, describe, and reason about decomposing, combining, and transforming polygons to make other polygons. Through building, drawing, and analyzing two-dimensional shapes, students understand attributes and properties of two-dimensional space and the use of those attributes and properties in solving problems, including applications involving congruence and symmetry.	***Algebra:*** Understanding properties of multiplication and the relationship between multiplication and division is a part of algebra readiness that develops at grade 3. The creation and analysis of patterns and relationships involving multiplication and division should occur at this grade level. Students build a foundation for later understanding of functional relationships by describing relationships in context with such statements as, "The number of legs is 4 times the number of chairs." ***Measurement:*** Students in grade 3 strengthen their understanding of fractions as they confront problems in linear measurement that call for more precision than the whole unit allowed them in their work in grade 2. They develop their facility in measuring with fractional parts of linear units. Students develop measurement concepts and skills through experiences in analyzing attributes and properties of two-dimensional objects. They form an understanding of perimeter as a measurable attribute and select appropriate units, strategies, and tools to solve problems involving perimeter. ***Data Analysis:*** Addition, subtraction, multiplication, and division of whole numbers come into play as students construct and analyze frequency tables, bar graphs, picture graphs, and line plots and use them to solve problems. ***Number and Operations:*** Building on their work in grade 2, students extend their understanding of place value to numbers up to 10,000 in various contexts. Students also apply this understanding to the task of representing numbers in different equivalent forms (e.g., expanded notation). They develop their understanding of numbers by building their facility with mental computation (addition and subtraction in special cases, such as 2,500 + 6,000 and 9,000 – 5,000), by using computational estimation, and by performing paper-and-pencil computations.

Curriculum Focal Points and Connections for Grade 4

The set of three curriculum focal points and related connections for mathematics in grade 4 follow. These topics are the recommended content emphases for this grade level. It is essential that these focal points be addressed in contexts that promote problem solving, reasoning, communication, making connections, and designing and analyzing representations.

Grade 4 Curriculum Focal Points	Connections to the Focal Points
***Number and Operations* and *Algebra:* Developing quick recall of multiplication facts and related division facts and fluency with whole number multiplication** Students use understandings of multiplication to develop quick recall of the basic multiplication facts and related division facts. They apply their understanding of models for multiplication (i.e., equal-sized groups, arrays, area models, equal intervals on the number line), place value, and properties of operations (in particular, the distributive property) as they develop, discuss, and use efficient, accurate, and generalizable methods to multiply multidigit whole numbers. They select appropriate methods and apply them accurately to estimate products or calculate them mentally, depending on the context and numbers involved. They develop fluency with efficient procedures, including the standard algorithm, for multiplying whole numbers, understand why the procedures work (on the basis of place value and properties of operations), and use them to solve problems. ***Number and Operations:* Developing an understanding of decimals, including the connections between fractions and decimals** Students understand decimal notation as an extension of the base-ten system of writing whole numbers that is useful for representing more numbers, including numbers between 0 and 1, between 1 and 2, and so on. Students relate their understanding of fractions to reading and writing decimals that are greater than or less than 1, identifying equivalent decimals, comparing and ordering decimals, and estimating decimal or fractional amounts in problem solving. They connect equivalent fractions and decimals by comparing models to symbols and locating equivalent symbols on the number line. ***Measurement:* Developing an understanding of area and determining the areas of two-dimensional shapes** Students recognize area as an attribute of two-dimensional regions. They learn that they can quantify area by finding the total number of same-sized units of area that cover the shape without gaps or overlaps. They understand that a square that is 1 unit on a side is the standard unit for measuring area. They select appropriate units, strategies (e.g., decomposing shapes), and tools for solving problems that involve estimating or measuring area. Students connect area measure to the area model that they have used to represent multiplication, and they use this connection to justify the formula for the area of a rectangle.	***Algebra:*** Students continue identifying, describing, and extending numeric patterns involving all operations and nonnumeric growing or repeating patterns. Through these experiences, they develop an understanding of the use of a rule to describe a sequence of numbers or objects. ***Geometry:*** Students extend their understanding of properties of two-dimensional shapes as they find the areas of polygons. They build on their earlier work with symmetry and congruence in grade 3 to encompass transformations, including those that produce line and rotational symmetry. By using transformations to design and analyze simple tilings and tessellations, students deepen their understanding of two-dimensional space. ***Measurement:*** As part of understanding two-dimensional shapes, students measure and classify angles. ***Data Analysis:*** Students continue to use tools from grade 3, solving problems by making frequency tables, bar graphs, picture graphs, and line plots. They apply their understanding of place value to develop and use stem-and-leaf plots. ***Number and Operations:*** Building on their work in grade 3, students extend their understanding of place value and ways of representing numbers to 100,000 in various contexts. They use estimation in determining the relative sizes of amounts or distances. Students develop understandings of strategies for multidigit division by using models that represent division as the inverse of multiplication, as partitioning, or as successive subtraction. By working with decimals, students extend their ability to recognize equivalent fractions. Students' earlier work in grade 3 with models of fractions and multiplication and division facts supports their understanding of techniques for generating equivalent fractions and simplifying fractions.

Curriculum Focal Points and Connections for Grade 5

The set of three curriculum focal points and related connections for mathematics in grade 5 follow. These topics are the recommended content emphases for this grade level. It is essential that these focal points be addressed in contexts that promote problem solving, reasoning, communication, making connections, and designing and analyzing representations.

Grade 5 Curriculum Focal Points

Number and Operations and *Algebra:* Developing an understanding of and fluency with division of whole numbers

Students apply their understanding of models for division, place value, properties, and the relationship of division to multiplication as they develop, discuss, and use efficient, accurate, and generalizable procedures to find quotients involving multidigit dividends. They select appropriate methods and apply them accurately to estimate quotients or calculate them mentally, depending on the context and numbers involved. They develop fluency with efficient procedures, including the standard algorithm, for dividing whole numbers, understand why the procedures work (on the basis of place value and properties of operations), and use them to solve problems. They consider the context in which a problem is situated to select the most useful form of the quotient for the solution, and they interpret it appropriately.

Number and Operations: Developing an understanding of and fluency with addition and subtraction of fractions and decimals

Students apply their understandings of fractions and fraction models to represent the addition and subtraction of fractions with unlike denominators as equivalent calculations with like denominators. They apply their understandings of decimal models, place value, and properties to add and subtract decimals. They develop fluency with standard procedures for adding and subtracting fractions and decimals. They make reasonable estimates of fraction and decimal sums and differences. Students add and subtract fractions and decimals to solve problems, including problems involving measurement.

Geometry and *Measurement* and *Algebra:* Describing three-dimensional shapes and analyzing their properties, including volume and surface area

Students relate two-dimensional shapes to three-dimensional shapes and analyze properties of polyhedral solids, describing them by the number of edges, faces, or vertices as well as the types of faces. Students recognize volume as an attribute of three-dimensional space. They understand that they can quantify volume by finding the total number of same-sized units of volume that they need to fill the space without gaps or overlaps. They understand that a cube that is 1 unit on an edge is the standard unit for measuring volume. They select appropriate units, strategies, and tools for solving problems that involve estimating or measuring volume. They decompose three-dimensional shapes and find surface areas and volumes of prisms. As they work with surface area, they find and justify relationships among the formulas for the areas of different polygons. They measure necessary attributes of shapes to use area formulas to solve problems.

Connections to the Focal Points

Algebra: Students use patterns, models, and relationships as contexts for writing and solving simple equations and inequalities. They create graphs of simple equations. They explore prime and composite numbers and discover concepts related to the addition and subtraction of fractions as they use factors and multiples, including applications of common factors and common multiples. They develop an understanding of the order of operations and use it for all operations.

Measurement: Students' experiences connect their work with solids and volume to their earlier work with capacity and weight or mass. They solve problems that require attention to both approximation and precision of measurement.

Data Analysis: Students apply their understanding of whole numbers, fractions, and decimals as they construct and analyze double-bar and line graphs and use ordered pairs on coordinate grids.

Number and Operations: Building on their work in grade 4, students extend their understanding of place value to numbers through millions and millionths in various contexts. They apply what they know about multiplication of whole numbers to larger numbers. Students also explore contexts that they can describe with negative numbers (e.g., situations of owing money or measuring elevations above and below sea level).

Curriculum Focal Points and Connections for Grade 6

The set of three curriculum focal points and related connections for mathematics in grade 6 follow. These topics are the recommended content emphases for this grade level. It is essential that these focal points be addressed in contexts that promote problem solving, reasoning, communication, making connections, and designing and analyzing representations.

Grade 6 Curriculum Focal Points

Number and Operations: **Developing an understanding of and fluency with multiplication and division of fractions and decimals**

Students use the meanings of fractions, multiplication and division, and the inverse relationship between multiplication and division to make sense of procedures for multiplying and dividing fractions and explain why they work. They use the relationship between decimals and fractions, as well as the relationship between finite decimals and whole numbers (i.e., a finite decimal multiplied by an appropriate power of 10 is a whole number), to understand and explain the procedures for multiplying and dividing decimals. Students use common procedures to multiply and divide fractions and decimals efficiently and accurately. They multiply and divide fractions and decimals to solve problems, including multistep problems and problems involving measurement.

Number and Operations: **Connecting ratio and rate to multiplication and division**

Students use simple reasoning about multiplication and division to solve ratio and rate problems (e.g., "If 5 items cost $3.75 and all items are the same price, then I can find the cost of 12 items by first dividing $3.75 by 5 to find out how much one item costs and then multiplying the cost of a single item by 12"). By viewing equivalent ratios and rates as deriving from, and extending, pairs of rows (or columns) in the multiplication table, and by analyzing simple drawings that indicate the relative sizes of quantities, students extend whole number multiplication and division to ratios and rates. Thus, they expand the repertoire of problems that they can solve by using multiplication and division, and they build on their understanding of fractions to understand ratios. Students solve a wide variety of problems involving ratios and rates.

Algebra: **Writing, interpreting, and using mathematical expressions and equations**

Students write mathematical expressions and equations that correspond to given situations, they evaluate expressions, and they use expressions and formulas to solve problems. They understand that variables represent numbers whose exact values are not yet specified, and they use variables appropriately. Students understand that expressions in different forms can be equivalent, and they can rewrite an expression to represent a quantity in a different way (e.g., to make it more compact or to feature different information). Students know that the solutions of an equation are the values of the variables that make the equation true. They solve simple one-step equations by using number sense, properties of operations, and the idea of maintaining equality on both sides of an equation. They construct and analyze tables (e.g., to show quantities that are in equivalent ratios), and they use equations to describe simple relationships (such as $3x = y$) shown in a table.

Connections to the Focal Points

Number and Operations: Students' work in dividing fractions shows them that they can express the result of dividing two whole numbers as a fraction (viewed as parts of a whole). Students then extend their work in grade 5 with division of whole numbers to give mixed number and decimal solutions to division problems with whole numbers. They recognize that ratio tables not only derive from rows in the multiplication table but also connect with equivalent fractions. Students distinguish multiplicative comparisons from additive comparisons.

Algebra: Students use the commutative, associative, and distributive properties to show that two expressions are equivalent. They also illustrate properties of operations by showing that two expressions are equivalent in a given context (e.g., determining the area in two different ways for a rectangle whose dimensions are $x + 3$ by 5). Sequences, including those that arise in the context of finding possible rules for patterns of figures or stacks of objects, provide opportunities for students to develop formulas.

Measurement and ***Geometry:*** Problems that involve areas and volumes, calling on students to find areas or volumes from lengths or to find lengths from volumes or areas and lengths, are especially appropriate. These problems extend the students' work in grade 5 on area and volume and provide a context for applying new work with equations.

Curriculum Focal Points and Connections for Grade 7

The set of three curriculum focal points and related connections for mathematics in grade 7 follow. These topics are the recommended content emphases for this grade level. It is essential that these focal points be addressed in contexts that promote problem solving, reasoning, communication, making connections, and designing and analyzing representations.

Grade 7 Curriculum Focal Points	Connections to the Focal Points
***Number and Operations* and *Algebra* and *Geometry:* Developing an understanding of and applying proportionality, including similarity** Students extend their work with ratios to develop an understanding of proportionality that they apply to solve single and multistep problems in numerous contexts. They use ratio and proportionality to solve a wide variety of percent problems, including problems involving discounts, interest, taxes, tips, and percent increase or decrease. They also solve problems about similar objects (including figures) by using scale factors that relate corresponding lengths of the objects or by using the fact that relationships of lengths within an object are preserved in similar objects. Students graph proportional relationships and identify the unit rate as the slope of the related line. They distinguish proportional relationships ($y/x = k$, or $y = kx$) from other relationships, including inverse proportionality ($xy = k$, or $y = k/x$). ***Measurement* and *Geometry* and *Algebra:* Developing an understanding of and using formulas to determine surface areas and volumes of three-dimensional shapes** By decomposing two- and three-dimensional shapes into smaller, component shapes, students find surface areas and develop and justify formulas for the surface areas and volumes of prisms and cylinders. As students decompose prisms and cylinders by slicing them, they develop and understand formulas for their volumes (*Volume* = *Area of base* × *Height*). They apply these formulas in problem solving to determine volumes of prisms and cylinders. Students see that the formula for the area of a circle is plausible by decomposing a circle into a number of wedges and rearranging them into a shape that approximates a parallelogram. They select appropriate two- and three-dimensional shapes to model real-world situations and solve a variety of problems (including multistep problems) involving surface areas, areas and circumferences of circles, and volumes of prisms and cylinders. ***Number and Operations* and *Algebra:* Developing an understanding of operations on all rational numbers and solving linear equations** Students extend understandings of addition, subtraction, multiplication, and division, together with their properties, to all rational numbers, including negative integers. By applying properties of arithmetic and considering negative numbers in everyday contexts (e.g., situations of owing money or measuring elevations above and below sea level), students explain why the rules for adding, subtracting, multiplying, and dividing with negative numbers make sense. They use the arithmetic of rational numbers as they formulate and solve linear equations in one variable and use these equations to solve problems. Students make strategic choices of procedures to solve linear equations in one variable and implement them efficiently, understanding that when they use the properties of equality to express an equation in a new way, solutions that they obtain for the new equation also solve the original equation.	***Measurement* and *Geometry:*** Students connect their work on proportionality with their work on area and volume by investigating similar objects. They understand that if a scale factor describes how corresponding lengths in two similar objects are related, then the square of the scale factor describes how corresponding areas are related, and the cube of the scale factor describes how corresponding volumes are related. Students apply their work on proportionality to measurement in different contexts, including converting among different units of measurement to solve problems involving rates such as motion at a constant speed. They also apply proportionality when they work with the circumference, radius, and diameter of a circle; when they find the area of a sector of a circle; and when they make scale drawings. ***Number and Operations:*** In grade 4, students used equivalent fractions to determine the decimal representations of fractions that they could represent with terminating decimals. Students now use division to express any fraction as a decimal, including fractions that they must represent with infinite decimals. They find this method useful when working with proportions, especially those involving percents. Students connect their work with dividing fractions to solving equations of the form $ax = b$, where a and b are fractions. Students continue to develop their understanding of multiplication and division and the structure of numbers by determining if a counting number greater than 1 is a prime, and if it is not, by factoring it into a product of primes. ***Data Analysis:*** Students use proportions to make estimates relating to a population on the basis of a sample. They apply percentages to make and interpret histograms and circle graphs. ***Probability:*** Students understand that when all outcomes of an experiment are equally likely, the theoretical probability of an event is the fraction of outcomes in which the event occurs. Students use theoretical probability and proportions to make approximate predictions.

Curriculum Focal Points and Connections for Grade 8

The set of three curriculum focal points and related connections for mathematics in grade 8 follow. These topics are the recommended content emphases for this grade level. It is essential that these focal points be addressed in contexts that promote problem solving, reasoning, communication, making connections, and designing and analyzing representations.

Grade 8 Curriculum Focal Points

***Algebra:* Analyzing and representing linear functions and solving linear equations and systems of linear equations**

Students use linear functions, linear equations, and systems of linear equations to represent, analyze, and solve a variety of problems. They recognize a proportion ($y/x = k$, or $y = kx$) as a special case of a linear equation of the form $y = mx + b$, understanding that the constant of proportionality (k) is the slope and the resulting graph is a line through the origin. Students understand that the slope (m) of a line is a constant rate of change, so if the input, or x-coordinate, changes by a specific amount, a, the output, or y-coordinate, changes by the amount ma. Students translate among verbal, tabular, graphical, and algebraic representations of functions (recognizing that tabular and graphical representations are usually only partial representations), and they describe how such aspects of a function as slope and y-intercept appear in different representations. Students solve systems of two linear equations in two variables and relate the systems to pairs of lines that intersect, are parallel, or are the same line, in the plane. Students use linear equations, systems of linear equations, linear functions, and their understanding of the slope of a line to analyze situations and solve problems.

***Geometry* and *Measurement:* Analyzing two- and three-dimensional space and figures by using distance and angle**

Students use fundamental facts about distance and angles to describe and analyze figures and situations in two- and three-dimensional space and to solve problems, including those with multiple steps. They prove that particular configurations of lines give rise to similar triangles because of the congruent angles created when a transversal cuts parallel lines. Students apply this reasoning about similar triangles to solve a variety of problems, including those that ask them to find heights and distances. They use facts about the angles that are created when a transversal cuts parallel lines to explain why the sum of the measures of the angles in a triangle is 180 degrees, and they apply this fact about triangles to find unknown measures of angles. Students explain why the Pythagorean theorem is valid by using a variety of methods—for example, by decomposing a square in two different ways. They apply the Pythagorean theorem to find distances between points in the Cartesian coordinate plane to measure lengths and analyze polygons and polyhedra.

***Data Analysis* and *Number and Operations* and *Algebra:* Analyzing and summarizing data sets**

Students use descriptive statistics, including mean, median, and range, to summarize and compare data sets, and they organize and display data to pose and answer questions. They compare the information provided by the mean and the median and investigate the different effects that changes in data values have on these measures of center. They understand that a measure of center alone does not thoroughly describe a data set because very different data sets can share the same measure of center. Students select the mean or the median as the appropriate measure of center for a given purpose.

Connections to the Focal Points

Algebra: Students encounter some nonlinear functions (such as the inverse proportions that they studied in grade 7 as well as basic quadratic and exponential functions) whose rates of change contrast with the constant rate of change of linear functions. They view arithmetic sequences, including those arising from patterns or problems, as linear functions whose inputs are counting numbers. They apply ideas about linear functions to solve problems involving rates such as motion at a constant speed.

Geometry: Given a line in a coordinate plane, students understand that all "slope triangles"—triangles created by a vertical "rise" line segment (showing the change in y), a horizontal "run" line segment (showing the change in x), and a segment of the line itself—are similar. They also understand the relationship of these similar triangles to the constant slope of a line.

Data Analysis: Building on their work in previous grades to organize and display data to pose and answer questions, students now see numerical data as an aggregate, which they can often summarize with one or several numbers. In addition to the median, students determine the 25th and 75th percentiles (1st and 3rd quartiles) to obtain information about the spread of data. They may use box-and-whisker plots to convey this information. Students make scatterplots to display bivariate data, and they informally estimate lines of best fit to make and test conjectures.

Number and Operations: Students use exponents and scientific notation to describe very large and very small numbers. They use square roots when they apply the Pythagorean theorem.

Appendix

A Comparison of the Curriculum Focal Points and Connections with the Expectations of the Content Standards in *Principles and Standards for School Mathematics*

Three tables follow that present side-by-side comparisons of the grade-level curriculum focal points and accompanying connections presented in this publication with the expectations of the Content Standards presented in *Principles and Standards for School Mathematics* (NCTM 2000). Each table encompasses a grade band: pre-K–grade 2, grades 3–5, or grades 6–8. The left-hand column in each grade-band table shows the curriculum focal points and corresponding connections presented in *Curriculum Focal Points for Prekindergarten through Grade 8 Mathematics* for all the grade levels in the grade band. Expectations from the Content Standards for the grade band appear in the right-hand column of each table. A link between an expectation on the right and content in a focal point or connection on the left is indicated by a dot in a color that specifies the relevant grade level. This color falls within a group of colors that represent all the grade levels in the relevant grade band.

The tables use the following colors to indicate content in *Principles and Standards* that appears in the focal points of particular grade levels:

- For the pre-K–2 grade band—
  - ● yellow indicates prekindergarten;
  - ● green indicates kindergarten;
  - ● red indicates grade 1;
  - ● blue indicates grade 2.
- For the 3–5 grade band—
  - ● yellow indicates grade 3;
  - ● green indicates grade 4;
  - ● red indicates grade 5.
- For the 6–8 grade band—
  - ● yellow indicates grade 6;
  - ● green indicates grade 7;
  - ● red indicates grade 8.

Readers should note that colors repeat in sequence from grade band to grade band.

Many expectations from the Content Standards are accompanied by multiple colored dots because these expectations specify developmental ideas that span several grade levels within a grade band. If a statement appears with more than one colored dot, the different colors indicate the multiple grade levels to which the statement is linked. Multiple dots beside a statement indicate that *some part of the statement appears in some form* in the focal points or connections of the grade levels that the colors represent.

By contrast, a very small number of expectations or their components are not identified by any grade-level color. This may occur for one of two reasons, with one of two results:

● Purple indicates content that appears in the focal points or connections of a grade level that is outside the grade band shown in a table.

○ White indicates content that is not identified as a focal point or connection at any grade level, pre-K–grade 8.

1. Occasionally, content from *Principles and Standards* appears in the curriculum focal points of a grade level that is not included in the grade band shown in a particular table. Such statements are indicated by dots in purple, a color that is different from all the colors representing levels in the grade band. The grade level where such content does appear in a focal point or connection is specified.
2. Content from *Principles and Standards* that does not appear in the curriculum focal points or connections of *any* grade level, prekindergarten through grade 8, appears with a white dot. Curriculum planners who use this framework in designing a mathematics program may add these few expectations from *Principles and Standards* to their curriculum at an appropriate grade level, pre-K–grade 8, or they can address these expectations in their mathematics program for grades 9–12.

The three tables in the appendix demonstrate that the curriculum focal points and connections presented in this publication are a direct application of the Content Standards in *Principles and Standards for School Mathematics* to the development of a focused and coherent mathematics curriculum for prekindergarten through grade 8. Effective implementation of these content emphases in the context of the processes addressed in the Process Standards in *Principles and Standards* (problem solving, reasoning and proof, communication, connections, and representation) can provide students with a challenging, high-quality mathematics program.

Table A.1. Pre-K–Grade 2 Curriculum Focal Points and Connections Compared with the Expectations of the Content Standards in *Principles and Standards for School Mathematics*

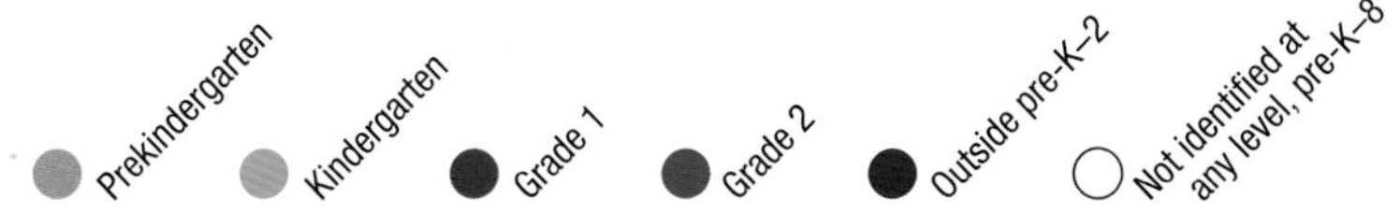

Curriculum Focal Points and Connections

Prekindergarten Curriculum Focal Points

***Number and Operations:* Developing an understanding of whole numbers, including concepts of correspondence, counting, cardinality, and comparison**

Children develop an understanding of the meanings of whole numbers and recognize the number of objects in small groups without counting and by counting—the first and most basic mathematical algorithm. They understand that number words refer to quantity. They use one-to-one correspondence to solve problems by matching sets and comparing number amounts and in counting objects to 10 and beyond. They understand that the last word that they state in counting tells "how many," they count to determine number amounts and compare quantities (using language such as "more than" and "less than"), and they order sets by the number of objects in them.

***Geometry:* Identifying shapes and describing spatial relationships**

Children develop spatial reasoning by working from two perspectives on space as they examine the shapes of objects and inspect their relative positions. They find shapes in their environments and describe them in their own words. They build pictures and designs by combining two- and three-dimensional shapes, and they solve such problems as deciding which piece will fit into a space in a puzzle. They discuss the relative positions of objects with vocabulary such as "above," "below," and "next to."

***Measurement:* Identifying measurable attributes and comparing objects by using these attributes**

Children identify objects as "the same" or "different," and then "more" or "less," on the basis of attributes that they can measure. They identify measurable attributes such as length and weight and solve problems by making direct comparisons of objects on the basis of those attributes.

Connections to the Prekindergarten Focal Points

Data Analysis: Children learn the foundations of data analysis by using objects' attributes that they have identified in relation to geometry and measurement (e.g., size, quantity, orientation, number of sides or vertices, color) for various purposes, such as describing, sorting, or comparing. For example, children sort geometric figures by shape, compare objects by weight ("heavier," "lighter"), or describe sets of objects by the number of objects in each set.

Expectations of the Content Standards

Number and Operations, Pre-K–Grade 2

Count with understanding and recognize "how many" in sets of objects

Use multiple models to develop initial understandings of place value and the base-ten number system

Develop understanding of the relative position and magnitude of whole numbers and of ordinal and cardinal numbers and their connections

Develop a sense of whole numbers and represent and use them in flexible ways, including relating, composing, and decomposing numbers

Connect number words and numerals to the quantities they represent, using various physical models and representations

Understand and represent commonly used fractions, such as 1/4, 1/3, and 1/2. [In Grade 3 Curriculum Focal Points]

Understand various meanings of addition and subtraction of whole numbers and the relationship between the two operations

Understand the effects of adding and subtracting whole numbers

Understand situations that entail multiplication and division, such as equal groupings of objects and sharing equally

Develop and use strategies for whole-number computations, with a focus on addition and subtraction

Develop fluency with basic number combinations for addition and subtraction

Use a variety of methods and tools to compute, including objects, mental computation, estimation, paper and pencil, and calculators

(Continued)

Prekindergarten · Kindergarten · Grade 1 · Grade 2 · Outside pre-K–2 · Not identified at any level, pre-K–8

Curriculum Focal Points and Connections

Prekindergarten Curriculum Focal Points

Connections to the Prekindergarten Focal Points

Number and Operations: Children use meanings of numbers to create strategies for solving problems and responding to practical situations, such as getting just enough napkins for a group, or mathematical situations, such as determining that any shape is a triangle if it has exactly three straight sides and is closed.

Algebra: Children recognize and duplicate simple sequential patterns (e.g., square, circle, square, circle, square, circle,...).

Kindergarten Curriculum Focal Points

***Number and Operation:* Representing, comparing, and ordering whole numbers and joining and separating sets**

Children use numbers, including written numerals, to represent quantities and to solve quantitative problems, such as counting objects in a set, creating a set with a given number of objects, comparing and ordering sets or numerals by using both cardinal and ordinal meanings, and modeling simple joining and separating situations with objects. They choose, combine, and apply effective strategies for answering quantitative questions, including quickly recognizing the number in a small set, counting and producing sets of given sizes, counting the number in combined sets, and counting backward.

***Geometry:* Describing shapes and space**

Children interpret the physical world with geometric ideas (e.g., shape, orientation, spatial relations) and describe it with corresponding vocabulary. They identify, name, and describe a variety of shapes, such as squares, triangles, circles, rectangles, (regular) hexagons, and (isosceles) trapezoids presented in a variety of ways (e.g., with different sizes or orientations), as well as such three-dimensional shapes as spheres, cubes, and cylinders. They use basic shapes and spatial reasoning to model objects in their environment and to construct more complex shapes.

***Measurement:* Ordering objects by measurable attributes**

Children use measurable attributes, such as length or weight, to solve problems by comparing and ordering objects. They compare the lengths of two objects both directly (by comparing them with each other) and indirectly (by comparing both with a third object), and they order several objects according to length.

Expectations of the Content Standards

Algebra, Pre-K–Grade 2

- Sort, classify, and order objects by size, number, and other properties
- Recognize, describe, and extend patterns such as sequences of sounds and shapes or simple numeric patterns and translate from one representation to another
- Analyze how both repeating and growing patterns are generated
- Illustrate general principles and properties of operations, such as commutativity, using specific numbers
- Use concrete, pictorial, and verbal representations to develop an understanding of invented and conventional symbolic notations
- Model situations that involve the addition and subtraction of whole numbers, using objects, pictures, and symbols
- Describe qualitative change, such as a student's growing taller
- Describe quantitative change, such as a student's growing two inches in one year

Geometry, Pre-K–Grade 2

- Recognize, name, build, draw, compare, and sort two- and three-dimensional shapes [Naming of three-dimensional shapes occurs in Grade 5 Curriculum Focal Points.]
- Describe attributes and parts of two- and three-dimensional shapes
- Investigate and predict the results of putting together and taking apart two- and three-dimensional shapes
- Describe, name, and interpret relative positions in space and apply ideas about relative position

(*Continued*)

Table A.1. (*Continued*)

Prekindergarten · Kindergarten · Grade 1 · Grade 2 · Outside pre-K–2 · Not identified at any level, pre-K–8

Curriculum Focal Points and Connections

Kindergarten Curriculum Focal Points

Connections to the Kindergarten Focal Points

Data Analysis: Children sort objects and use one or more attributes to solve problems. For example, they might sort solids that roll easily from those that do not. Or they might collect data and use counting to answer such questions as, "What is our favorite snack?" They re-sort objects by using new attributes (e.g., after sorting solids according to which ones roll, they might re-sort the solids according to which ones stack easily).

Geometry: Children integrate their understandings of geometry, measurement, and number. For example, they understand, discuss, and create simple navigational directions (e.g., "Walk forward 10 steps, turn right, and walk forward 5 steps").

Algebra: Children identify, duplicate, and extend simple number patterns and sequential and growing patterns (e.g., patterns made with shapes) as preparation for creating rules that describe relationships.

Grade 1 Curriculum Focal Points

Number and Operations **and** ***Algebra:*** **Developing understandings of addition and subtraction and strategies for basic addition facts and related subtraction facts**

Children develop strategies for adding and subtracting whole numbers on the basis of their earlier work with small numbers. They use a variety of models, including discrete objects, length-based models (e.g., lengths of connecting cubes), and number lines, to model "part-whole," "adding to," "taking away from," and "comparing" situations to develop an understanding of the meanings of addition and subtraction and strategies to solve such arithmetic problems. Children understand the connections between counting and the operations of addition and subtraction (e.g., adding two is the same as "counting on" two). They use properties of addition (commutativity and associativity) to add whole numbers, and they create and use increasingly sophisticated strategies based on these properties (e.g., "making tens") to solve addition and subtraction problems involving basic facts. By comparing a variety of solution strategies, children relate addition and subtraction as inverse operations.

Expectations of the Content Standards

Geometry, Pre-K–Grade 2 *(Continued)*

- Describe, name, and interpret direction and distance in navigating space and apply ideas about direction and distance
- Find and name locations with simple relationships such as "near to" and in coordinate systems such as maps [This use of coordinate systems is not identified as a focal point or connection.]
- Recognize and apply slides, flips, and turns [In Grade 4 Curriculum Focal Points]
- Recognize and create shapes that have symmetry
- Create mental images of geometric shapes using spatial memory and spatial visualization
- Recognize and represent shapes from different perspectives
- Relate ideas in geometry to ideas in number and measurement
- Recognize geometric shapes and structures in the environment and specify their location

Measurement, Pre-K–Grade 2

- Recognize the attributes of length, volume, weight, area, and time [Time is not identified as a focal point or connection.]
- Compare and order objects according to these attributes
- Understand how to measure using nonstandard and standard units
- Select an appropriate unit and tool for the attribute being measured
- Measure with multiple copies of units of the same size, such as paper clips laid end to end

(*Continued*)

● Prekindergarten ● Kindergarten ● Grade 1 ● Grade 2 ● Outside pre-K–2 ○ Not identified at any level, pre-K–8

Curriculum Focal Points and Connections

Grade 1 Curriculum Focal Points

***Number and Operations:* Developing an understanding of whole number relationships, including grouping in tens and ones**

Children compare and order whole numbers (at least to 100) to develop an understanding of and solve problems involving the relative sizes of these numbers. They think of whole numbers between 10 and 100 in terms of groups of tens and ones (especially recognizing the numbers 11 to 19 as 1 group of ten and particular numbers of ones). They understand the sequential order of the counting numbers and their relative magnitudes and represent numbers on a number line.

***Geometry:* Composing and decomposing geometric shapes**

Children compose and decompose plane and solid figures (e.g., by putting two congruent isosceles triangles together to make a rhombus), thus building an understanding of part-whole relationships as well as the properties of the original and composite shapes. As they combine figures, they recognize them from different perspectives and orientations, describe their geometric attributes and properties, and determine how they are alike and different, in the process developing a background for measurement and initial understandings of such properties as congruence and symmetry.

Connections to the Grade 1 Focal Points

Number and Operations and ***Algebra:*** Children use mathematical reasoning, including ideas such as commutativity and associativity and beginning ideas of tens and ones, to solve two-digit addition and subtraction problems with strategies that they understand and can explain. They solve both routine and nonroutine problems.

Measurement and ***Data Analysis:*** Children strengthen their sense of number by solving problems involving measurements and data. Measuring by laying multiple copies of a unit end to end and then counting the units by using groups of tens and ones supports children's understanding of number lines and number relationships. Representing measurements and discrete data in picture and bar graphs involves counting and comparisons that provide another meaningful connection to number relationships.

Algebra: Through identifying, describing, and applying number patterns and properties in developing strategies for basic facts, children learn about other properties of numbers and operations, such as odd and even (e.g., "Even numbers of objects can be paired, with none left over"), and 0 as the identity element for addition.

Expectations of the Content Standards

Measurement, Pre-K–Grade 2 *(Continued)*

- ● (Grade 1) Use repetition of a single unit to measure something larger than the unit, for instance, measuring the length of a room with a single meterstick
- ● (Grade 1) Use tools to measure
- ● (Grade 1) Develop common referents for measures to make comparisons and estimates

Data Analysis and Probability, Pre-K–Grade 2

- ● (Kindergarten) Pose questions and gather data about themselves and their surroundings
- ● ● ● (Prekindergarten, Kindergarten, Grade 1) Sort and classify objects according to their attributes and organize data about the objects
- ● (Grade 1) Represent data using concrete objects, pictures, and graphs
- ● ● (Prekindergarten, Grade 1) Describe parts of the data and the set of data as a whole to determine what the data show
- ● (Outside pre-K–2) Discuss events related to students' experiences as likely or unlikely [In Grade 7 Curriculum Focal Points]

(Continued)

Table A.1. (*Continued*)

Prekindergarten · Kindergarten · Grade 1 · Grade 2 · Outside pre-K–2 · Not identified at any level, pre-K–8

Curriculum Focal Points and Connections	Expectations of the Content Standards

Grade 2 Curriculum Focal Points

***Number and Operations:* Developing an understanding of the base-ten numeration system and place-value concepts**

Children develop an understanding of the base-ten numeration system and place-value concepts (at least to 1000). Their understanding of base-ten numeration includes ideas of counting in units and multiples of hundreds, tens, and ones, as well as a grasp of number relationships, which they demonstrate in a variety of ways, including comparing and ordering numbers. They understand multidigit numbers in terms of place value, recognizing that place-value notation is a shorthand for the sums of multiples of powers of 10 (e.g., 853 as 8 hundreds + 5 tens + 3 ones).

Number and Operations and ***Algebra:* Developing quick recall of addition facts and related subtraction facts and fluency with multidigit addition and subtraction**

Children use their understanding of addition to develop quick recall of basic addition facts and related subtraction facts. They solve arithmetic problems by applying their understanding of models of addition and subtraction (such as combining or separating sets or using number lines), relationships and properties of number (such as place value), and properties of addition (commutativity and associativity). Children develop, discuss, and use efficient, accurate, and generalizable methods to add and subtract multidigit whole numbers. They select and apply appropriate methods to estimate sums and differences or calculate them mentally, depending on the context and numbers involved. They develop fluency with efficient procedures, including standard algorithms, for adding and subtracting whole numbers, understand why the procedures work (on the basis of place value and properties of operations), and use them to solve problems.

***Measurement:* Developing an understanding of linear measurement and facility in measuring lengths**

Children develop an understanding of the meaning and processes of measurement, including such underlying concepts as partitioning (the mental activity of slicing the length of an object into equal-sized units) and transitivity (e.g., if object A is longer than object B and object B is longer than object C, then object A is longer than object C). They understand linear measure as an iteration of units and use rulers and other measurement tools with that understanding. They understand the need for equal-length

(*Continued*)

Prekindergarten | Kindergarten | Grade 1 | Grade 2 | Outside pre-K–2 | Not identified at any level, pre-K–8

Curriculum Focal Points and Connections	Expectations of the Content Standards

Grade 2 Curriculum Focal Points

units, the use of standard units of measure (centimeter and inch), and the inverse relationship between the size of a unit and the number of units used in a particular measurement (i.e., children recognize that the smaller the unit, the more iterations they need to cover a given length).

Connections to Grade 2 Focal Points

Number and Operations: Children use place value and properties of operations to create equivalent representations of given numbers (such as 35 represented by 35 ones, 3 tens and 5 ones, or 2 tens and 15 ones) and to write, compare, and order multidigit numbers. They use these ideas to compose and decompose multidigit numbers. Children add and subtract to solve a variety of problems, including applications involving measurement, geometry, and data, as well as nonroutine problems. In preparation for grade 3, they solve problems involving multiplicative situations, developing initial understandings of multiplication as repeated addition.

Geometry and ***Measurement:*** Children estimate, measure, and compute lengths as they solve problems involving data, space, and movement through space. By composing and decomposing two-dimensional shapes (intentionally substituting arrangements of smaller shapes for larger shapes or substituting larger shapes for many smaller shapes), they use geometric knowledge and spatial reasoning to develop foundations for understanding area, fractions, and proportions.

Algebra: Children use number patterns to extend their knowledge of properties of numbers and operations. For example, when skip counting, they build foundations for understanding multiples and factors.

Table A.2. Grades 3–5 Curriculum Focal Points and Connections Compared with the Expectations of the Content Standards in *Principles and Standards for School Mathematics*

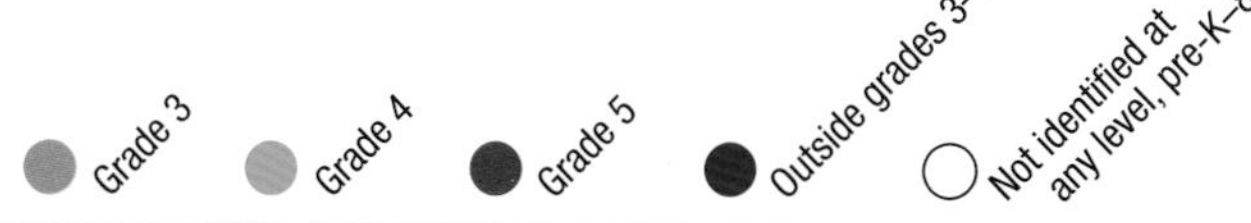

Curriculum Focal Points and Connections

Grade 3 Curriculum Focal Points

Number and Operations **and** ***Algebra:*** **Developing understandings of multiplication and division and strategies for basic multiplication facts and related division facts**

Students understand the meanings of multiplication and division of whole numbers through the use of representations (e.g., equal-sized groups, arrays, area models, and equal "jumps" on number lines for multiplication, and successive subtraction, partitioning, and sharing for division). They use properties of addition and multiplication (e.g., commutativity, associativity, and the distributive property) to multiply whole numbers and apply increasingly sophisticated strategies based on these properties to solve multiplication and division problems involving basic facts. By comparing a variety of solution strategies, students relate multiplication and division as inverse operations.

Number and Operations: **Developing an understanding of fractions and fraction equivalence**

Students develop an understanding of the meanings and uses of fractions to represent parts of a whole, parts of a set, or points or distances on a number line. They understand that the size of a fractional part is relative to the size of the whole, and they use fractions to represent numbers that are equal to, less than, or greater than 1. They solve problems that involve comparing and ordering fractions by using models, benchmark fractions, or common numerators or denominators. They understand and use models, including the number line, to identify equivalent fractions.

Geometry: **Describing and analyzing properties of two-dimensional shapes**

Students describe, analyze, compare, and classify two-dimensional shapes by their sides and angles and connect these attributes to definitions of shapes. Students investigate, describe, and reason about decomposing, combining, and transforming polygons to make other polygons. Through building, drawing, and analyzing two-dimensional shapes, students understand attributes and properties of two-dimensional space and the use of those attributes and properties in solving problems, including applications involving congruence and symmetry.

Expectations of the Content Standards

Number and Operations, Grades 3–5

Understand the place-value structure of the base-ten number system and be able to represent and compare whole numbers and decimals

Recognize equivalent representations for the same number and generate them by decomposing and composing numbers

Develop understanding of fractions as parts of unit wholes, as parts of a collection, as locations on number lines, and [in Grade 6 Curriculum Focal Points] as divisions of whole numbers

Use models, benchmarks, and equivalent forms to judge the size of fractions

Recognize and generate equivalent forms of commonly used fractions, decimals, and [in Grade 7 Curriculum Focal Points] percents

Explore numbers less than 0 by extending the number line and through familiar applications

Describe classes of numbers according to characteristics such as the nature of their factors

Understand various meanings of multiplication and division

Understand the effects of multiplying and dividing whole numbers

Identify and use relationships between operations, such as division as the inverse of multiplication, to solve problems

Understand and use properties of operations, such as the distributivity of multiplication over addition

Develop fluency with basic number combinations for multiplication and division and use these combinations to mentally compute related problems, such as 30×50

(Continued)

Table A.2. (*Continued*)

Grade 3 · Grade 4 · Grade 5 · Outside grades 3–5 · Not identified at any level, pre-K–8

Curriculum Focal Points and Connections

Grade 3 Curriculum Focal Points

Connections to Grade 3 Focal Points

Algebra: Understanding properties of multiplication and the relationship between multiplication and division is a part of algebra readiness that develops at grade 3. The creation and analysis of patterns and relationships involving multiplication and division should occur at this grade level. Students build a foundation for later understanding of functional relationships by describing relationships in context with such statements as, "The number of legs is 4 times the number of chairs."

Measurement: Students in grade 3 strengthen their understanding of fractions as they confront problems in linear measurement that call for more precision than the whole unit allowed them in their work in grade 2. They develop their facility in measuring with fractional parts of linear units. Students develop measurement concepts and skills through experiences in analyzing attributes and properties of two-dimensional objects. They form an understanding of perimeter as a measurable attribute and select appropriate units, strategies, and tools to solve problems involving perimeter.

Data Analysis: Addition, subtraction, multiplication, and division of whole numbers come into play as students construct and analyze frequency tables, bar graphs, picture graphs, and line plots and use them to solve problems.

Number and Operations: Building on their work in grade 2, students extend their understanding of place value to numbers up to 10,000 in various contexts. Students also apply this understanding to the task of representing numbers in different equivalent forms (e.g., expanded notation). They develop their understanding of numbers by building their facility with mental computation (addition and subtraction in special cases, such as 2,500 + 6,000 and 9,000 – 5,000), by using computational estimation, and by performing paper-and-pencil computations.

Grade 4 Curriculum Focal Points

Number and Operations and ***Algebra:*** **Developing quick recall of multiplication facts and related division facts and fluency with whole number multiplication**

Students use understandings of multiplication to develop quick recall of the basic multiplication facts and related division facts. They apply their understanding of models for multiplication (i.e., equal-sized groups, arrays, area models, equal intervals on the

Expectations of the Content Standards

Number and Operations, Grades 3–5 (*Continued*)

Develop fluency in adding, subtracting, multiplying, and dividing whole numbers

Develop and use strategies to estimate the results of whole-number computations and to judge the reasonableness of such results

Develop and use strategies to estimate computations involving fractions and decimals in situations relevant to students' experience

Use visual models, benchmarks, and equivalent forms to add and subtract commonly used fractions and decimals

Select appropriate methods and tools for computing with whole numbers from among mental computation, estimation, calculators, and paper and pencil according to the context and nature of the computation and use the selected method or tool

Algebra, Grades 3–5

Describe, extend, and make generalizations about geometric and numeric patterns

Represent and analyze patterns and functions, using words, tables, and graphs

Identify such properties as commutativity, associativity, and distributivity and use them to compute with whole numbers

Represent the idea of a variable as an unknown quantity using a letter or a symbol [In Grade 6 Curriculum Focal Points]

Express mathematical relationships using equations

Model problem situations with objects and use representations such as graphs, tables, and equations to draw conclusions

(*Continued*)

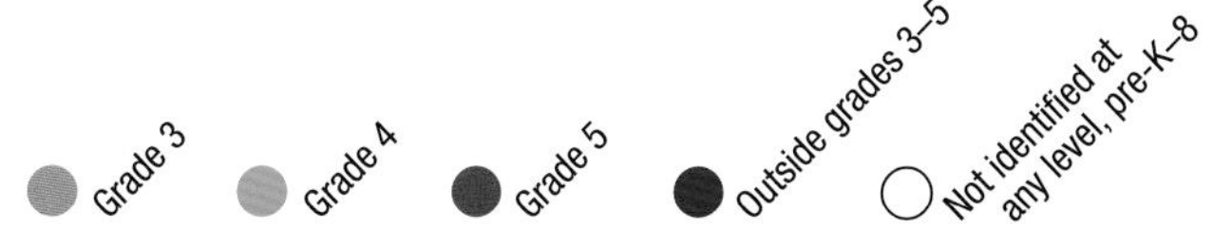

Curriculum Focal Points and Connections

Grade 4 Curriculum Focal Points

number line), place value, and properties of operations (in particular, the distributive property) as they develop, discuss, and use efficient, accurate, and generalizable methods to multiply multidigit whole numbers. They select appropriate methods and apply them accurately to estimate products or calculate them mentally, depending on the context and numbers involved. They develop fluency with efficient procedures, including the standard algorithm, for multiplying whole numbers, understand why the procedures work (on the basis of place value and properties of operations), and use them to solve problems.

***Number and Operations:* Developing an understanding of decimals, including the connections between fractions and decimals**

Students understand decimal notation as an extension of the base-ten system of writing whole numbers that is useful for representing more numbers, including numbers between 0 and 1, between 1 and 2, and so on. Students relate their understanding of fractions to reading and writing decimals that are greater than or less than 1, identifying equivalent decimals, comparing and ordering decimals, and estimating decimal or fractional amounts in problem solving. They connect equivalent fractions and decimals by comparing models to symbols and locating equivalent symbols on the number line.

***Measurement:* Developing an understanding of area and determining the areas of two-dimensional shapes**

Students recognize area as an attribute of two-dimensional regions. They learn that they can quantify area by finding the total number of same-sized units of area that cover the shape without gaps or overlaps. They understand that a square that is 1 unit on a side is the standard unit for measuring area. They select appropriate units, strategies (e.g., decomposing shapes), and tools for solving problems that involve estimating or measuring area. Students connect area measure to the area model that they have used to represent multiplication, and they use this connection to justify the formula for the area of a rectangle.

Connections to Grade 4 Focal Points

Algebra: Students continue identifying, describing, and extending numeric patterns involving all operations and nonnumeric growing or repeating patterns. Through these experiences, they develop an understanding of the use of a rule to describe a sequence of numbers or objects.

Expectations of the Content Standards

***Algebra, Grades 3–5** (Continued)*

- Investigate how a change in one variable relates to a change in a second variable [In Grade 7 Curriculum Focal Points]
- Identify and describe situations with constant or varying rates of change and compare them [In Grade 7 Curriculum Focal Points]

Geometry, Grades 3–5

- Identify, compare, and analyze attributes of two- and three-dimensional shapes and develop vocabulary to describe the attributes
- Classify two- and three-dimensional shapes according to their properties and develop definitions of classes of shapes such as triangles and pyramids
- Investigate, describe, and reason about the results of subdividing, combining, and transforming shapes
- Explore congruence and similarity
- Make and test conjectures about geometric properties and relationships and develop logical arguments to justify conclusions
- Describe location and movement using common language and geometric vocabulary
- Make and use coordinate systems to specify locations and to describe paths
- Find the distance between points along horizontal and vertical lines of a coordinate system
- Predict and describe the results of sliding, flipping, and turning two-dimensional shapes

(Continued)

Grade 3 · Grade 4 · Grade 5 · Outside grades 3–5 · Not identified at any level, pre-K–8

Curriculum Focal Points and Connections

Grade 4 Curriculum Focal Points

Connections to Grade 4 Focal Points

Geometry: Students extend their understanding of properties of two-dimensional shapes as they find the areas of polygons. They build on their earlier work with symmetry and congruence in grade 3 to encompass transformations, including those that produce line and rotational symmetry. By using transformations to design and analyze simple tilings and tessellations, students deepen their understanding of two-dimensional space.

Measurement: As part of understanding two-dimensional shapes, students measure and classify angles.

Data Analysis: Students continue to use tools from grade 3, solving problems by making frequency tables, bar graphs, picture graphs, and line plots. They apply their understanding of place value to develop and use stem-and-leaf plots.

Number and Operations: Building on their work in grade 3, students extend their understanding of place value and ways of representing numbers to 100,000 in various contexts. They use estimation in determining the relative sizes of amounts or distances. Students develop understandings of strategies for multidigit division by using models that represent division as the inverse of multiplication, as partitioning, or as successive subtraction. By working with decimals, students extend their ability to recognize equivalent fractions. Students' earlier work in grade 3 with models of fractions and multiplication and division facts supports their understanding of techniques for generating equivalent fractions and simplifying fractions.

Grade 5 Curriculum Focal Points

Number and Operations and ***Algebra:*** **Developing an understanding of and fluency with division of whole numbers**

Students apply their understanding of models for division, place value, properties, and the relationship of division to multiplication as they develop, discuss, and use efficient, accurate, and generalizable procedures to find quotients involving multidigit dividends. They select appropriate methods and apply them accurately to estimate quotients or calculate them mentally, depending on the context and numbers involved. They develop fluency with efficient procedures, including the standard algorithm, for dividing whole numbers, understand why the procedures work (on the basis of place value and proper-

Expectations of the Content Standards

Geometry, Grades 3–5 (*Continued*)

- Describe a motion or a series of motions that will show that two shapes are congruent
- Identify and describe line and rotational symmetry in two- and three-dimensional shapes and designs
- Build and draw geometric objects
- Create and describe mental images of objects, patterns, and paths
- Identify and build a three-dimensional object from two-dimensional representations of that object
- Identify and draw a two-dimensional representation of a three-dimensional object
- Use geometric models to solve problems in other areas of mathematics, such as number and measurement
- Recognize geometric ideas and relationships and apply them to other disciplines and to problems that arise in the classroom or in everyday life

Measurement, Grades 3–5

- Understand such attributes as length, area, weight [identified in Grades 1 and 2 Curriculum Focal Points], volume, and size of angle and select the appropriate type of unit for measuring each attribute
- Understand the need for measuring with standard units and become familiar with standard units in the customary and metric systems
- Carry out simple unit conversions, such as from centimeters to meters, within a system of measurement
- Understand that measurements are approximations and understand how differences in units affect precision

(*Continued*)

Grade 3 · Grade 4 · Grade 5 · Outside grades 3–5 · Not identified at any level, pre-K–8

Curriculum Focal Points and Connections

Grade 5 Curriculum Focal Points

ties of operations), and use them to solve problems. They consider the context in which a problem is situated to select the most useful form of the quotient for the solution, and they interpret it appropriately.

***Number and Operations:* Developing an understanding of and fluency with addition and subtraction of fractions and decimals**

Students apply their understandings of fractions and fraction models to represent the addition and subtraction of fractions with unlike denominators as equivalent calculations with like denominators. They apply their understandings of decimal models, place value, and properties to add and subtract decimals. They develop fluency with standard procedures for adding and subtracting fractions and decimals. They make reasonable estimates of fraction and decimal sums and differences. Students add and subtract fractions and decimals to solve problems, including problems involving measurement.

***Geometry* and *Measurement* and *Algebra:* Describing three-dimensional shapes and analyzing their properties, including volume and surface area**

Students relate two-dimensional shapes to three-dimensional shapes and analyze properties of polyhedral solids, describing them by the number of edges, faces, or vertices as well as the types of faces. Students recognize volume as an attribute of three-dimensional space. They understand that they can quantify volume by finding the total number of same-sized units of volume that they need to fill the space without gaps or overlaps. They understand that a cube that is 1 unit on an edge is the standard unit for measuring volume. They select appropriate units, strategies, and tools for solving problems that involve estimating or measuring volume. They decompose three-dimensional shapes and find surface areas and volumes of prisms. As they work with surface area, they find and justify relationships among the formulas for the areas of different polygons. They measure necessary attributes of shapes to use area formulas to solve problems.

Connections to Grade 5 Focal Points

Algebra: Students use patterns, models, and relationships as contexts for writing and solving simple equations and inequalities. They create graphs of simple equations. They explore prime and composite numbers and discover concepts related to the addition and subtraction of fractions as they use factors and multiples, including applications of

Expectations of the Content Standards

Measurement, Grades 3–5 *(Continued)*

Markers	Expectation
Grade 3, Grade 4	Explore what happens to measurements of a two-dimensional shape such as its perimeter and area when the shape is changed in some way
Grade 3, Grade 4, Grade 5	Develop strategies for estimating the perimeters, areas, and volumes of irregular shapes
Grade 3, Grade 4, Grade 5, Not identified	Select and apply appropriate standard units and tools to measure length, area, volume, weight, time, temperature, and the size of angles [Measuring time and temperature is not identified as a focal point or connection.]
Grade 3, Grade 4, Grade 5, Outside grades 3–5	Select and use benchmarks to estimate measurements [Also in Grade 2 Curriculum Focal Points]
Grade 4	Develop, understand, and use formulas to find the area of rectangles and related triangles and parallelograms
Grade 5	Develop strategies to determine the surface areas and volumes of rectangular solids

Data Analysis and Probability, Grades 3–5

Markers	Expectation
Grade 3, Grade 4, Grade 5	Design investigations to address a question and consider how data-collection methods affect the nature of the data set
Grade 3, Grade 4, Grade 5	Collect data using observations, surveys, and experiments
Grade 3, Grade 4, Grade 5	Represent data using tables and graphs such as line plots, bar graphs, and line graphs
Grade 5	Recognize the differences in representing categorical and numerical data

(*Continued*)

Grade 3 · Grade 4 · Grade 5 · Outside grades 3–5 · Not identified at any level, pre-K–8

Curriculum Focal Points and Connections

Grade 5 Curriculum Focal Points

Connections to Grade 5 Focal Points

common factors and common multiples. They develop an understanding of the order of operations and use it for all operations.

Measurement: Students' experiences connect their work with solids and volume to their earlier work with capacity and weight or mass. They solve problems that require attention to both approximation and precision of measurement.

Data Analysis: Students apply their understanding of whole numbers, fractions, and decimals as they construct and analyze double-bar and line graphs and use ordered pairs on coordinate grids.

Number and Operations: Building on their work in grade 4, students extend their understanding of place value to numbers through millions and millionths in various contexts. They apply what they know about multiplication of whole numbers to larger numbers. Students also explore contexts that they can describe with negative numbers (e.g., situations of owing money or measuring elevations above and below sea level).

Expectations of the Content Standards

Data Analysis and Probability, Grades 3–5 *(Continued)*

Describe the shape and important features of a set of data and compare related data sets, with [in Grade 8 Curriculum Focal Points] an emphasis on how the data are distributed

Use measures of center, focusing on the median, and understand what each does and does not indicate about the data set [In Grade 8 Curriculum Focal Points]

Compare different representations of the same data and evaluate how well each representation shows important aspects of the data [Also in Grade 8 Curriculum Focal Points]

Propose and justify conclusions and predictions that are based on data and design studies to further investigate the conclusions or predictions [Designing such studies is not identified as a focal point or connection.]

Describe events as likely or unlikely and discuss the degree of likelihood using such words as *certain, equally likely,* and *impossible* [In Grade 7 Curriculum Focal Points]

Predict the probability of outcomes of simple experiments and test the predictions [in Grade 7 Curriculum Focal Points]

Understand that the measure of the likelihood of an event can be represented by a number from 0 to 1 [In Grade 7 Curriculum Focal Points]

Table A.3. Grades 6–8 Curriculum Focal Points and Connections Compared with the Expectations of the Content Standards in *Principles and Standards for School Mathematics*

Grade 6 · Grade 7 · Grade 8 · Outside grades 6–8 · Not identified at any level, pre-K–8

Curriculum Focal Points and Connections

Grade 6 Curriculum Focal Points

***Number and Operations:* Developing an understanding of and fluency with multiplication and division of fractions and decimals**

Students use the meanings of fractions, multiplication and division, and the inverse relationship between multiplication and division to make sense of procedures for multiplying and dividing fractions and explain why they work. They use the relationship between decimals and fractions, as well as the relationship between finite decimals and whole numbers (i.e., a finite decimal multiplied by an appropriate power of 10 is a whole number), to understand and explain the procedures for multiplying and dividing decimals. Students use common procedures to multiply and divide fractions and decimals efficiently and accurately. They multiply and divide fractions and decimals to solve problems, including multistep problems and problems involving measurement.

***Number and Operations:* Connecting ratio and rate to multiplication and division**

Students use simple reasoning about multiplication and division to solve ratio and rate problems (e.g., "If 5 items cost $3.75 and all items are the same price, then I can find the cost of 12 items by first dividing $3.75 by 5 to find out how much one item costs and then multiplying the cost of a single item by 12"). By viewing equivalent ratios and rates as deriving from, and extending, pairs of rows (or columns) in the multiplication table, and by analyzing simple drawings that indicate the relative sizes of quantities, students extend whole number multiplication and division to ratios and rates. Thus, they expand the repertoire of problems that they can solve by using multiplication and division, and they build on their understanding of fractions to understand ratios. Students solve a wide variety of problems involving ratios and rates.

***Algebra:* Writing, interpreting, and using mathematical expressions and equations**

Students write mathematical expressions and equations that correspond to given situations, they evaluate expressions, and they use expressions and formulas to solve problems. They understand that variables represent numbers whose exact values are not yet specified, and they use variables appropriately. Students understand that expressions in different forms can be equivalent, and they can rewrite an expression to represent a quantity in a different way (e.g., to make it more compact or to feature different information). Students know that the solutions of an equation are the values of the variables that

Expectations of the Content Standards

Number and Operations, Grades 6–8

- Work flexibly with fractions, decimals, and percents to solve problems
- Compare and order fractions, decimals, and percents efficiently and find their approximate locations on a number line
- Develop meaning for percents greater than 100 and less than 1
- Understand and use ratios and proportions to represent quantitative relationships
- Develop an understanding of large numbers [identified in Grades 4 and 5 Curriculum Focal Points] and recognize and appropriately use exponential, scientific, and calculator notation
- Use factors, multiples, prime factorization, and relatively prime numbers to solve problems
- Develop meaning for integers and represent and compare quantities with them
- Understand the meaning and effects of arithmetic operations with fractions, decimals, and integers
- Use the associative and commutative properties of addition and multiplication and the distributive property of multiplication over addition to simplify computations with integers, fractions, and decimals
- Understand and use the inverse relationships of addition and subtraction, multiplication and division, and squaring and finding square roots to simplify computations and solve problems
- Select appropriate methods and tools for computing with fractions and decimals from among mental computation, estimation, calculators or computers, and paper and pencil, depending on the situation, and apply the selected methods

(Continued)

Grade 6 · Grade 7 · Grade 8 · Outside grades 6–8 · Not identified at any level, pre-K–8

Curriculum Focal Points and Connections

Grade 6 Curriculum Focal Points

make the equation true. They solve simple one-step equations by using number sense, properties of operations, and the idea of maintaining equality on both sides of an equation. They construct and analyze tables (e.g., to show quantities that are in equivalent ratios), and they use equations to describe simple relationships (such as $3x = y$) shown in a table.

Connections to Grade 6 Focal Points

Number and Operations: Students' work in dividing fractions shows them that they can express the result of dividing two whole numbers as a fraction (viewed as parts of a whole). Students then extend their work in grade 5 with division of whole numbers to give mixed number and decimal solutions to division problems with whole numbers. They recognize that ratio tables not only derive from rows in the multiplication table but also connect with equivalent fractions. Students distinguish multiplicative comparisons from additive comparisons.

Algebra: Students use the commutative, associative, and distributive properties to show that two expressions are equivalent. They also illustrate properties of operations by showing that two expressions are equivalent in a given context (e.g., determining the area in two different ways for a rectangle whose dimensions are $x + 3$ by 5). Sequences, including those that arise in the context of finding possible rules for patterns of figures or stacks of objects, provide opportunities for students to develop formulas.

Measurement and ***Geometry:*** Problems that involve areas and volumes, calling on students to find areas or volumes from lengths or to find lengths from volumes or areas and lengths, are especially appropriate. These problems extend the students' work in grade 5 on area and volume and provide a context for applying new work with equations.

Grade 7 Curriculum Focal Points

Number and Operations **and** ***Algebra*** **and** ***Geometry:*** **Developing an understanding of and applying proportionality, including similarity**

Students extend their work with ratios to develop an understanding of proportionality that they apply to solve single and multistep problems in numerous contexts. They use

Expectations of the Content Standards

Number and Operations, Grades 6–8 *(Continued)*

- Develop and analyze algorithms for computing with fractions, decimals, and integers and develop fluency in their use
- Develop and use strategies to estimate the results of rational-number computations and judge the reasonableness of the results
- Develop, analyze, and explain methods for solving problems involving proportions, such as scaling and finding equivalent ratios

Algebra, Grades 6–8

- Represent, analyze, and generalize a variety of patterns with tables, graphs, words, and, when possible, symbolic rules
- Relate and compare different forms of representation for a relationship
- Identify functions as linear or nonlinear and contrast their properties from tables, graphs, or equations
- Develop an initial conceptual understanding of different uses of variables
- Explore relationships between symbolic expressions and graphs of lines, paying particular attention to the meaning of intercept and slope
- Use symbolic algebra to represent situations and to solve problems, especially those that involve linear relationships
- Recognize and generate equivalent forms for simple algebraic expressions and solve linear equations
- Model and solve contextualized problems using various representations, such as graphs, tables, and equations

(Continued)

Table A.3. (*Continued*)

Grade 6 · Grade 7 · Grade 8 · Outside grades 6–8 · Not identified at any level, pre-K–8

Curriculum Focal Points and Connections

Grade 7 Curriculum Focal Points

ratio and proportionality to solve a wide variety of percent problems, including problems involving discounts, interest, taxes, tips, and percent increase or decrease. They also solve problems about similar objects (including figures) by using scale factors that relate corresponding lengths of the objects or by using the fact that relationships of lengths within an object are preserved in similar objects. Students graph proportional relationships and identify the unit rate as the slope of the related line. They distinguish proportional relationships ($y/x = k$, or $y = kx$) from other relationships, including inverse proportionality ($xy = k$, or $y = k/x$).

***Measurement* and *Geometry* and *Algebra:* Developing an understanding of and using formulas to determine surface areas and volumes of three-dimensional shapes**

By decomposing two- and three-dimensional shapes into smaller, component shapes, students find surface areas and develop and justify formulas for the surface areas and volumes of prisms and cylinders. As students decompose prisms and cylinders by slicing them, they develop and understand formulas for their volumes (*Volume* = *Area of base* × *Height*). They apply these formulas in problem solving to determine volumes of prisms and cylinders. Students see that the formula for the area of a circle is plausible by decomposing a circle into a number of wedges and rearranging them into a shape that approximates a parallelogram. They select appropriate two- and three-dimensional shapes to model real-world situations and solve a variety of problems (including multistep problems) involving surface areas, areas and circumferences of circles, and volumes of prisms and cylinders.

***Number and Operations* and *Algebra:* Developing an understanding of operations on all rational numbers and solving linear equations**

Students extend understandings of addition, subtraction, multiplication, and division, together with their properties, to all rational numbers, including negative integers. By applying properties of arithmetic and considering negative numbers in everyday contexts (e.g., situations of owing money or measuring elevations above and below sea level), students explain why the rules for adding, subtracting, multiplying, and dividing with negative numbers make sense. They use the arithmetic of rational numbers as they formulate and solve linear equations in one variable and use these equations to solve problems. Students make strategic choices of procedures to solve linear equations in one

Expectations of the Content Standards

Algebra, Grades 6–8 (*Continued*)

- Use graphs to analyze the nature of changes in quantities in linear relationships

Geometry, Grades 6–8

- Precisely describe, classify, and understand relationships among types of two- and three-dimensional objects using their defining properties
- Understand relationships among the angles, side lengths, perimeters, areas, and volumes of similar objects
- Create and critique inductive and deductive arguments concerning geometric ideas and relationships, such as congruence, similarity, and the Pythagorean relationship
- Use coordinate geometry to represent and examine the properties of geometric shapes [Also in Grade 5 Curriculum Focal Points]
- Use coordinate geometry to examine special geometric shapes, such as regular polygons or those with pairs of parallel or perpendicular sides
- Describe sizes, positions, and orientations of shapes under informal transformations such as flips, turns, slides [these transformations are identified in Grade 4 Curriculum Focal Points], and scaling
- Examine the congruence, similarity, and line or rotational symmetry of objects using transformations [In Grade 4 Curriculum Focal Points]
- Draw geometric objects with specified properties, such as side lengths or angle measures
- Use two-dimensional representations of three-dimensional objects to visualize and solve problems such as those involving surface area and volume

(Continued)

Table A.3. (*Continued*)

Grade 6 · Grade 7 · Grade 8 · Outside grades 6–8 · Not identified at any level, pre-K–8

Curriculum Focal Points and Connections

Grade 7 Curriculum Focal Points

variable and implement them efficiently, understanding that when they use the properties of equality to express an equation in a new way, solutions that they obtain for the new equation also solve the original equation.

Connections to Grade 7 Focal Points

Measurement and ***Geometry:*** Students connect their work on proportionality with their work on area and volume by investigating similar objects. They understand that if a scale factor describes how corresponding lengths in two similar objects are related, then the square of the scale factor describes how corresponding areas are related, and the cube of the scale factor describes how corresponding volumes are related. Students apply their work on proportionality to measurement in different contexts, including converting among different units of measurement to solve problems involving rates such as motion at a constant speed. They also apply proportionality when they work with the circumference, radius, and diameter of a circle; when they find the area of a sector of a circle; and when they make scale drawings.

Number and Operations: In grade 4, students used equivalent fractions to determine the decimal representations of fractions that they could represent with terminating decimals. Students now use division to express any fraction as a decimal, including fractions that they must represent with infinite decimals. They find this method useful when working with proportions, especially those involving percents. Students connect their work with dividing fractions to solving equations of the form $ax = b$, where a and b are fractions. Students continue to develop their understanding of multiplication and division and the structure of numbers by determining if a counting number greater than 1 is a prime, and if it is not, by factoring it into a product of primes.

Data Analysis: Students use proportions to make estimates relating to a population on the basis of a sample. They apply percentages to make and interpret histograms and circle graphs.

Probability: Students understand that when all outcomes of an experiment are equally likely, the theoretical probability of an event is the fraction of outcomes in which the event occurs. Students use theoretical probability and proportions to make approximate predictions.

Expectations of the Content Standards

Geometry, Grades 6–8 (*Continued*)

Use visual tools such as networks to represent and solve problems [Networks are not identified as focal points or connections.]

Use geometric models to represent and explain numerical and algebraic relationships

Recognize and apply geometric ideas and relationships in areas outside the mathematics classroom, such as art, science, and everyday life

Measurement, Grades 6–8

Understand both metric and customary systems of measurement

Understand relationships among units and convert from one unit to another within the same system

Understand, select, and use units of appropriate size and type to measure angles, perimeter, area, surface area, and volume

Use common benchmarks to select appropriate methods for estimating measurements [In Grades 3–5 Curriculum Focal Points]

Select and apply techniques and tools to accurately find length, area, volume, and angle measures to appropriate levels of precision

Develop and use formulas to determine the circumference of circles and the area of triangles, parallelograms, trapezoids, and circles and develop strategies to find the area of more-complex shapes

Develop strategies to determine the surface area and volume of selected prisms, pyramids, and cylinders

Solve problems involving scale factors, using ratio and proportion

Solve simple problems involving rates and derived measurements for such attributes as velocity and density

(*Continued*)

Grade 6 | Grade 7 | Grade 8 | Outside grades 6–8 | Not identified at any level, pre-K–8

Curriculum Focal Points and Connections

Grade 8 Curriculum Focal Points

Algebra: Analyzing and representing linear functions and solving linear equations and systems of linear equations

Students use linear functions, linear equations, and systems of linear equations to represent, analyze, and solve a variety of problems. They recognize a proportion ($y/x = k$, or $y = kx$) as a special case of a linear equation of the form $y = mx + b$, understanding that the constant of proportionality (k) is the slope and the resulting graph is a line through the origin. Students understand that the slope (m) of a line is a constant rate of change, so if the input, or x-coordinate, changes by a specific amount, a, the output, or y-coordinate, changes by the amount ma. Students translate among verbal, tabular, graphical, and algebraic representations of functions (recognizing that tabular and graphical representations are usually only partial representations), and they describe how such aspects of a function as slope and y-intercept appear in different representations. Students solve systems of two linear equations in two variables and relate the systems to pairs of lines that intersect, are parallel, or are the same line, in the plane. Students use linear equations, systems of linear equations, linear functions, and their understanding of the slope of a line to analyze situations and solve problems.

Geometry and Measurement: Analyzing two- and three-dimensional space and figures by using distance and angle

Students use fundamental facts about distance and angles to describe and analyze figures and situations in two- and three-dimensional space and to solve problems, including those with multiple steps. They prove that particular configurations of lines give rise to similar triangles because of the congruent angles created when a transversal cuts parallel lines. Students apply this reasoning about similar triangles to solve a variety of problems, including those that ask them to find heights and distances. They use facts about the angles that are created when a transversal cuts parallel lines to explain why the sum of the measures of the angles in a triangle is 180 degrees, and they apply this fact about triangles to find unknown measures of angles. Students explain why the Pythagorean theorem is valid by using a variety of methods—for example, by decomposing a square in two different ways. They apply the Pythagorean theorem to find distances between points in the Cartesian coordinate plane to measure lengths and analyze polygons and polyhedra.

Expectations of the Content Standards

Data Analysis and Probability, Grades 6–8

- (Grade 7) Formulate questions, design studies, and collect data about a characteristic shared by two populations or different characteristics within one population
- (Grade 8 / Outside grades 6–8) Select, create, and use appropriate graphical representations of data, including histograms, box plots, and scatterplots
- (Grade 8 / Outside grades 6–8) Find, use, and interpret measures of center and spread, including mean and interquartile range
- (Grade 8 / Outside grades 6–8) Discuss and understand the correspondence between data sets and their graphical representations, especially histograms, stem-and-leaf plots, box plots, and scatterplots
- (Grade 8 / Outside grades 6–8) Use observations about differences between two or more samples to make conjectures about the populations from which the samples were taken
- (Grade 8 / Outside grades 6–8) Make conjectures about possible relationships between two characteristics of a sample on the basis of scatterplots of the data and approximate lines of fit
- (Grade 8 / Outside grades 6–8) Use conjectures to formulate new questions and plan new studies to answer them
- (Not identified) Understand and use appropriate terminology to describe complementary and mutually exclusive events
- (Grade 8 / Outside grades 6–8) Use proportionality and a basic understanding of probability to make and test conjectures about the results of experiments and simulations
- (Not identified) Compute probabilities for simple compound events, using such methods as organized lists, tree diagrams, and area models

(*Continued*)

Grade 6 · Grade 7 · Grade 8 · Outside grades 6–8 · Not identified at any level, pre-K–8

Curriculum Focal Points and Connections	Expectations of the Content Standards

Grade 8 Curriculum Focal Points

Data Analysis **and *Number and Operations* and *Algebra:* Analyzing and summarizing data sets**

Students use descriptive statistics, including mean, median, and range, to summarize and compare data sets, and they organize and display data to pose and answer questions. They compare the information provided by the mean and the median and investigate the different effects that changes in data values have on these measures of center. They understand that a measure of center alone does not thoroughly describe a data set because very different data sets can share the same measure of center. Students select the mean or the median as the appropriate measure of center for a given purpose.

Grade 8 Curriculum Focal Points

Algebra: Students encounter some nonlinear functions (such as the inverse proportions that they studied in grade 7 as well as basic quadratic and exponential functions) whose rates of change contrast with the constant rate of change of linear functions. They view arithmetic sequences, including those arising from patterns or problems, as linear functions whose inputs are counting numbers. They apply ideas about linear functions to solve problems involving rates such as motion at a constant speed.

Geometry: Given a line in a coordinate plane, students understand that all "slope triangles"—triangles created by a vertical "rise" line segment (showing the change in y), a horizontal "run" line segment (showing the change in x), and a segment of the line itself—are similar. They also understand the relationship of these similar triangles to the constant slope of a line.

Data Analysis: Building on their work in previous grades to organize and display data to pose and answer questions, students now see numerical data as an aggregate, which they can often summarize with one or several numbers. In addition to the median, students determine the 25th and 75th percentiles (1st and 3rd quartiles) to obtain information about the spread of data. They may use box-and-whisker plots to convey this information. Students make scatterplots to display bivariate data, and they informally estimate lines of best fit to make and test conjectures.

Number and Operations: Students use exponents and scientific notation to describe very large and very small numbers. They use square roots when they apply the Pythagorean theorem.

References

National Council of Teachers of Mathematics (NCTM). *An Agenda for Action.* Reston, Va.: NCTM, 1980.

———. *Curriculum and Evaluation Standards for School Mathematics.* Reston, Va.: NCTM, 1989.

———. *Professional Standards for Teaching Mathematics.* Reston, Va.: NCTM, 1991.

———. *Assessment Standards for School Mathematics.* Reston, Va.: NCTM, 1995.

———. *Principles and Standards for School Mathematics.* Reston, Va.: NCTM, 2000.

No Child Left Behind Act of 2001. Public Law 107-110. 107th Cong., 1st sess. 8 January 2002.

Reys, Barbara J., Shannon Dingman, Melissa McNaught, Troy P. Regis, and Junko Togashi. *What Mathematics Are Fourth Graders in the U.S. Expected to Learn?* Columbia, Mo.: University of Missouri, Center for the Study of Mathematics Curriculum, 2006.

Reys, Barbara J., Shannon Dingman, Angela Sutter, and Dawn Teuscher. *Development of State-Level Mathematics Curriculum Documents: Report of a Survey.* Columbia, Mo.: University of Missouri, Center for the Study of Mathematics Curriculum, 2005. Also available online at http://www.mathcurriculumcenter.org/resources/ASSMReport.pdf.

Schmidt, William H., Curtis C. McKnight, and Senta A. Raizen. *A Splintered Vision: An Investigation of U.S. Science and Mathematics Education.* Dordrecht, The Netherlands: Kluwer, 1997.